'VERSITY C

Schemes for Classroom Drama

Schemes for Classroom Drama

Maggie Hulson

Trentham Books

Stoke on Trent, UK and Sterling, USA

Trentham Books Limited

Westview House   22883 Quicksilver Drive
734 London Road   Sterling
Oakhill   VA 20166-2012
Stoke on Trent   USA
Staffordshire
England ST4 5NP

First published 2006

British Library Cataloguing-in-Publication Data
A catalogue record for this book is available from the
British Library

ISBN-10: 1-85856-376-3
ISBN-13: 978-1-85856-376-3

Every effort has been made to trace and acknowledge the sources of the art work reprinted here. We would welcome advice of any we have been unable to identify and will give them due acknowledgment.

pages 52/53: The Peopling of London pack extracts from the Museum of London (Refuge SoW)

pages 54/55: The photographs from 'Your War, Our Lives' the Amnesty pack (Refuge SoW)

page 79: The photograph of the female US soldier with Iraqi prisoner (Facility Sow)

Designed and typeset by Trentham Print Design Ltd., Chester and printed in Great Britain by Bemrose Shafron (Printers) Ltd., Chester

Contents

'I love the unanswered question, the unresolved story, the unclimbed mountain, the tender shard of an incomplete dream. Most of the time. But is it mandatory for a writer to be ambiguous about everything? Isn't it true that there have been fearful episodes in human history when prudence and discretion would just have been euphemisms for pusillanimity? When caution was actually cowardice? When sophistication was disguised decadence? When circumspection was really a kind of espousal?

Isn't it true, or at least theoretically possible, that there are times in the life of a people or a nation when the political climate demands that we – even the most unsophisticated of us – overtly take sides? I believe that such times are upon us.'

Arundhati Roy (2002) Shall We Leave it to the Experts? in *Another World is Possible*

Acknowledgements

Any writer must owe much to her predecessors. Where I am consciousness of an influence I have acknowledged it; but as my work has been growing for a period of more than 20 years in the company of others, I can only hope that I have not presented as my own that which belongs to another.

I would like to thank the following for their highly valued contributions to the matter of this book.

First and foremost, all the children and young people who have worked so imaginatively and generously with me over the years, and who have made the work as it made them.

My students for giving me permission to publish aspects of their work.

My patient editor, Gillian Klein for her much appreciated counsel and the gift of opportunity.

Guy Williams, for his warm encouragement and insightful scrutiny of my work over a number of years.

Margaret Higgins, chair of the National Association for the Teaching of Drama, for her succour and reassurance.

My colleagues:

- Hazel for taking and printing photographs and Imelda for searching,

- Lincoln and Chris for their technological know-how,

- Cormac for scientific advice

- And many others who have supported and encouraged my endeavours, both in school and at NATD workshops.

Theatr Powys, for inviting me to work alongside them and allowing me to publish the photographs of *The King, the Crow, and the Girl*.

Xeni Berisha, for facilitating and translating.

Qemail Dusica, Ardian Hajdari, Mejreme Berisha and all the teachers in Gjilan who have made me so welcome.

The Museum of London.

Amnesty International.

Naomi Doyle.

Dijana Milosevec, director of DAH Theatre Company, for permission to use the photograph of our school production, performed in Belgrade in December 2002.

Kyle for initiating me into a whole new world of digital photography.

My friends Paul, for his generous technical support, and Janey, for the poem and inspirations.

My mother for diligent proof-reading.

My lovely Alice, for her understanding, and unquestioning faith that I would be able to meet the deadline.

Family and friends for their interest and nourishment.

Finally, I would like to acknowledge the powerful influence of the late Tony Grady, a wonderful teacher. His endorsement meant a great deal.

Section One

**Introduction
Stories for Humans**

Introduction

This book is for drama teachers working in schools. It is born out of a daily practice, and has evolved over more than 20 years of teaching in the inner city. For the most part it provides detailed schemes of work, some of which have been have been used again and again, whilst others are more recent. The schemes are set out for easy use, with resource lists and suggestions for additional resources. Each of these schemes of work has been taught to young people in secondary schools, and as each scheme has unfolded it has been adapted and revised according to what the children have revealed they need to know.

The schemes refer to sources and influences, and these in turn indicate stance – that educational endeavour must centre itself on the needs of the learner, see the child as a 'questioning, competent and creative member of society'[1], and that the curriculum should be a humanising one.

The work in this book stands, firmly I hope, on the shoulders of Dorothy Heathcote, Gavin Bolton, Jerome Bruner, Geoff Gillham, and the movers and shakers in the National Association for the Teaching of Drama. Bertolt Brecht, Edward Bond, Lev Vygotsky and the ensuing work of Harry Daniels and Alex Kozulin have also been a significant influence.

Alongside each scheme of work are notes for the teacher explaining some of the thinking behind the approach, and highlighting particular aspects of drama teaching.

Section 1 *The Human Narrative* outlines an approach to the selection and adaptation of story for the creation of schemes of work.

Section 2 offers schemes of work for Key Stage 3. *Prometheus*, alongside *Stating the Obvious* draws out links between classroom drama and world events. It features a table that outlines the curriculum contents and contains notes on storytelling for the teacher.

The Song was originally devised for Black History Month, and makes links with history as well as with other art forms.

The Cooks in the Kitchen focuses on teaching in role and whole class Drama, and also provides a curriculum contents page.

Refuge demonstrates how the living experience of our young people can be acknowledged within a protective fiction, and pays particular attention to guided reflection and the need for contradiction.

Cassandra offers key elements of whole class drama teaching plus some commentary from teachers on the moment-to-moment unfolding of the drama

In *The Facility* the physicalisation and representations of the material world are emboldened and the theatrical moments that can underpin the teaching underlined.

Section 3 offers schemes of work for Key Stage 4. *What's Theatre For?* is designed for GCSE Drama students. It juxtaposes extracts from two texts, with the world of the drama student in school, and other actors outside of school. It raises questions about the purpose of theatre. It works both on text and off text.

The Crusades was written for year 11 GCSE Drama students, approaching the final unit of the OCR Drama GCSE Examination. For this unit the students are required to work as devisers, designers, directors and performers. While this work was going on the news was full of the threats of war against Iraq.

Guernica was developed from *The Crusades* scheme and is designed for year 10 students.

Gilgamesh marks a further development of integrating Drama with Dance and Music for the OCR Expressive Arts GCSE. It offers observations from teaching the SoW, some of which are treated as story. It contains a curriculum contents table.

The children and young people I have worked with, the colleagues and the workshop participants have all become part of the fabric of each scheme – a crucial part. They are not just out of the head of one person but out of the practice of many.

Thus in sections 2 and 3 this book aims to encourage classroom teachers to use and develop learning material and also a teaching methodology that strives to place the being of the class, and the students' development, at the centre of the work.

Section 4 suggests the wider context for drama teachers, as developed out of the classroom practice and stance presented here. For example, in section 2, *Stating the Obvious* demonstrates how it is possible to acknowledge and embrace world events within classroom, teaching about them at the same time as they impact on the being of young people. At the beginning of section 4 *Possibilities in Such Times* offers a way for teachers to support such learning across the curriculum.

The Teacher and TIE outlines the depth of learning that can take place when the classroom teacher works alongside theatre in education practitioners in the classroom.

The schemes of work in Sections 2 and 3 are also part of a struggle to develop a coherent Drama curriculum. The purpose of *Notes on a Connective Curriculum*, in Section 4, is to demonstrate how it is practically possible, by shaping a particular kind of curriculum, to challenge the skills based approach that can seem so seductive and approachable to beleaguered classroom practitioners by shaping a particular kind of curriculum. It offers for discussion a connective curriculum, and raises questions for the future orientation of drama teachers.

Note

1 Publicity material for the annual conference of The National Association for the Teaching of Drama 2005

Drama in the Classroom

Educational drama is essentially two things. It is an artistic social learning process that generates imaginative and reasoned activity, and it is an artistic social learning process managed by one teacher for a class of students.

At its most dynamic it is a large group experience, inviting the participants to engage in communal expression and shared understanding. This communality is further emphasised by the opportunity for authentic and direct participation in the learning process for both teacher and pupil.

Such a highly developed pedagogy requires teachers to be in many different places at once, as well as at the holding centre. Not only is the teacher engaged in an active process of striving to see with the children's eyes, but they *must* also see each child through a professional lens, and, at the same time, shape the whole collective experience.

Stories for Humans

The Many Threads – A Story that is True

Once upon a time there was a traveller. She travelled far from her home, on a quest driven by her charges. Her charges were back home, but they travelled everywhere with her too. It could not be otherwise. She journeyed to discover and to understand what it is to teach. Or rather, what it is to teach children – children who come every day to the same adults in the same place – adults who will shape their imagination and their reason.

One day the traveller was in the back of a van in England. She had come to this country because she had heard that it was the home, the wellspring of a very special way of teaching – a way that took all and held all. Also in the back of the van was a young drama teacher, just starting out. They were both on the road to a conference. They got talking. They asked each other what they knew and what it was they hoped for. The traveller began to speak of the children on whose behalf she quested.

This was a story the young teacher was never to forget.

'I teach children' the traveller said, 'who can neither see nor hear.'

The young teacher was nonplussed.

'How?' she said, and

'How can it be 'children' and not 'child'? Hard enough to teach one, I think – impossible to teach more'.

'Yes, you'd think so' said the traveller 'I teach a group of them.'

A moment of hysteria flooded the young teacher's senses. She thought of her struggles to manage classes of the able-bodied.

'How?' she insisted.

'With rope' the traveller said 'Many pieces of rope.'

The young teacher waited.

'It begins with a piece of rope around the waist of each child, and the other around my forearm. This way I can manage four on each arm – a group of eight children. Of course, the children can be frightened and difficult to begin with – and the rope has to have the right pliability- but over time we establish a series of rope signals and I begin to be able to manage them as a class.'

The young teacher was gripped, impressed.

'Of course,' the traveller continued, ' this means that the children are very teacher dependent.'

'How could it be otherwise?' the young teacher said.

'Yes, well – that's the question I have to answer' the traveller said,

'And I have made a start – you see, it's no good if they don't communicate with each other as well as with me – they need to learn from one another, and in some ways, they will learn things from each other that I can never teach them. I have found' the traveller said 'that if I detach the end of the rope that is around my arm, and tie it to the waist of another child, then the two connected children have to work things out together. Of course, it is a long, painstaking process, and the rope must be both soft and strong, but now – well, they begin to play together.'

The young teacher could not speak – she could see and hear, but, in that moment, she could not speak. Imagination was in conference with experience.

A Series of Rope Signals

The process of educational drama rests fundamentally on the social formation of the mind. We are essentially social beings whose brains are communally evolved organisms. We have only to study the documented cases of feral children, for example, young humans who develop outside, or on the boundaries of, human culture, to see this clearly demonstrated. It is not just that these wild children have no apparent understanding of acceptable human behaviour – they are also unable to speak. In fact, unless they are discovered when they are still very young, they never will learn to speak as a human being. If one cannot communicate as a human, one cannot think as a human. Language and thought go hand in hand.

Our social bonding is at the centre of our survival as a species – from the measured communal pace of pack hunters to the glory of, say, *Ballet Rambert* or the teamwork of rescue workers, we are social animals. We are dependent upon, formed by, and active in the creation of, the social environment, and we are organically imprinted so to do. This general genetic law of cultural development was, most memorably, formulated by the developmental psychologist L.S. Vygotsky, who found that 'Social relations or relations among people genetically underlie all higher functions and their relationships' (1981, p6).

This concept underpins another Vygotskian concept central to educational drama – the zone of proximal development. Harry Daniels (1996, p4) has defined this as

> The distance between a child's 'actual developmental level as determined by independent problem solving' and the higher level of 'potential development as determined through problem solving (Vygotsky, 1978) under adult guidance or in collaboration with more capable peers.

Educational drama can foster a highly particular zone of proximal development (ZPD). It invites pupils to enter into a fictional social setting in order to explore and learn from what they encounter there. As it unfolds it demonstrates interactive social behaviour with the work pursued at a conscious and unconscious level, evaluated as it progresses, both within and outside the fiction. In this way it enables pupils to move between their actual developmental levels whilst they are both participant and audience. This dual role of the 'do-er' and the 'see-er' enables them to observe, act and reflect as part of a continuous process, and because it is within an acknowledged fiction, it brings an added domain of consciousness, providing rich possibilities for the relationship between the individual and the social.

Such richness stems in part from educational drama's ability to create and offer up for manipulation the all-important pivot upon which the ZPD can turn. As the teacher selects signs, symbol, action, stories and contradictions she is stimulating the interests and emotions of the class so that, as Tag McEntagart (1981, p48) observed, their 'strongest wish and uppermost impulse is to want to make sense of the meaning for themselves'.

A Practical Example

A class has been told the beginning of the legend of the Minotaur. The themes in this story concern matters between parent and child, king and people; between darkness and light, knowing and not knowing, between truthfulness and lies.

The class are asked to take on the role of the builders of the labyrinth of Minos, King of ancient Crete. Their teacher is in role as the foreman. The teacher brings the children to a large piece of paper with the outline of the labyrinth sketched upon it. The only clear detail marked is the position of the gates.

Teacher in role congratulates them on their hard work and invites them to contribute to making the map of the labyrinth. This map is, she says, being made to acknowledge their hard work, and to

> honour those that have died in the making of this labyrinth – this place of darkness – as soon as we have made our map it must be destroyed – King's orders – the paths that thread this labyrinth must remain forever secret – but we have a brief time now to share what it is we know – I know that each

one of you has laboured in a different sector of this place – what can you tell me of it?

The builders recount and then draw what they have built. The teacher in role listens to their stories. She acknowledges them, accepting what they say, and reacting appropriately to the tenor of their tales. If there is doubt of authenticity other builders can be referred to. Each story or detail is added to the map. Piece by piece the class are creating a shared understanding of what the labyrinth contains. This is the starting point for several weeks of drama lessons.

The pivot here is the map – a representation of the creation of a place from a myth. Perhaps it is also an artistic 'ideal form' (Kozulin, 1998, p55), enabling the class to socially experiment with the essence of that which the labyrinth contains. The class provide the details. And what the class provides and the manner in which they provide it will inform the teacher of several things about the class – e.g. what they see as frightening, influences from the world they live in outside the classroom, and where they are setting their boundaries. Thus she will be able to manage the development of their work appropriately. And remember – the clearest detail she provided was about the gates – there is always the possibility of an exit.

While the pupils work in this way they can observe each other as their daily selves, and at the same time as 'others'. They are both children and builders, reacting to other children/builders. Also, they can see their teacher as her self, consciously being an 'other' in a role, which may illuminate both her stance as a teacher and their social and individual relationships to her. It enables them to watch an adult make artistic choices and select action. The children can participate at their own level in the company of their peers who are participating at their levels, and with their teacher as a guide within the drama, leading them, challenging them, structuring their work individually and collectively.

Whatever the tasks planned and placed by the teacher, she has to manage, however consciously, an unfolding moment-to-moment series of events. She has, simultaneously, to respond to and plot the course of the lesson as it happens, within a whole class context. She has not only to raise scaffolding for learning but also 'de-scaffold' the elements that hamper learning. A kind of negative or shadow scaffold. Both kinds of scaffolding must be stable enough to protect and sustain, and at the same time supple enough to adapt or transform at a moment's notice. As she moves through the lesson the teacher is in a constant process of strengthening some aspects of the scaffolding, and re-building others in response to the classes' individual and collective response to the lesson. It is not a matter of scaffolding simply for the individual child but also for the class, in relation to each other and to the teacher.

It begins with a piece of rope

With what, then, does the teacher connect the pupils, not just to herself but each one to the other?

In a story we have the power to write our world because the telling of stories enables us to pattern reality and vice versa. It is not so much that we are engaging in a conscious act of will to create a reality; it's more that we are engaged in a social process that both reflects and builds the cultural world in which we live. As we tell the story we are 'telling' reality – it makes *us* as we make *it*.

There are two forms of story that I have found to afford highly particular opportunities in the drama classroom – myths or legends, and real historical (and sometimes historicised) events. Both can lend themselves to epic treatment and to the conjecture lent by distance.

When selecting a myth, we are examining forces that influence cause and effect. The epic hero is fixed in time and place. His story is a given. He cannot do otherwise. Cassandra will pour out her prophecies and the Trojan War will be lost to the Greeks. Gilgamesh will bring about the destruction of Enkidu. This fixedness refers us to the material world, in both content and form. The very fact that there are givens bears a relationship to the material world that bounds our existence. At the same time, the appearances of the nature of the givens are there to be questioned. There are certain events

that *have* taken place, those who know the truth *have* gone unheeded and wars *are* fought, and it would appear that the central characters who caused these things to happen will go on in this way indefinitely. But by placing key framing questions, we can structure the drama so that the assessment of the object by the pupils enhances their understanding and questioning of the world.

Brecht placed one such question well:

A WORKER READS HISTORY

Who built the seven gates of Thebes?
The books are filled with the names of Kings
Was it kings who hauled the craggy blocks of stone?
And Babylon, so many times destroyed,
Who built the city up each time? In which of Lima's houses
That city glittering with gold, lived those who built it?
In the evening when the Chinese wall was finished
Where did the masons go?..........
.... So many particulars
So many questions.

Bertolt Brecht

By placing this order of question the drama can create another discourse, one that seeks not simply to look at life but to ask how it came to be this way.

The Right Pliability

What factors, then, influence us in the choosing and placing of story? What rules apply?

Edward Bond (2005) asserts that:

Reality is. It exists. Humanness is not. It is created. It does not generate itself. Humanness cannot be created unless inhumanness may be created. If there is truth a lie must be possible.

This is a core principle: the story must offer up possibilities for the creation of humanness – or its opposite. This principle is the left hand twist of the yarn, forming the strongest strand running through the rope. Against this the other strands are twisted and held.

There are other strands to plait around the common central one:

- A being coming into humanness – this can be a child, an adult, a werewolf
- Inhumanness – actual or potential
- A story that has stood the test of time – it contains the past, present and possible of which Bruner (1991) speaks.
- Contradictive normativity – Bruner (1996, p94) maintains that narratives are profoundly and inescapably normative, that is, that the narrative pre-supposes a claim about how one ought to be. There are also contradictions to explore
- A meaning that lends itself to being opened out, in relation to the material world

I illustrate the weaving of these strands through some discussion of schemes of work contained in this book.

■ *A being coming into humanness*

The inclusion of this element is associated with the classic structure of characters that change during story, with the additional feature of the innocence or ignorance of the not (fully) human. It is a common belief that stories for children should contain child characters, as children relish stories about themselves. I have found that adults too like to work along these boundaries i.e. where the individual and their culture (culture as Bruner defines it) are making and encountering each other. I think the notion that the adult is a finished child gives us a false view of childhood. The relationship between the individual and culture is a constant process – children and adults exist along the same continuum.

I was first drawn to *Gilgamesh* by the simple fact that it was written before the bible. The strongest pull was of the then, now and future of it. However, as I worked on the scheme I lost my sense of it. The more intellectual ideological pull palled. I went back over previous schemes which I had created and came to the conclusion that the problem with the story was that there was no child in it; as soon as I had

that thought the very next one was that of course there is a child – Enkidu. He takes the place of the child – through his induction into society we learn about the individual and the society. As the class explores the self and otherness in Enkidu they are researching and refining what it is to be human. Further down the line I saw what I should have seen from the outset – that Gilgamesh is the being learning how to be a human, and in Enkidu we see his mirror.

■ *Inhumanness*

Human development, indeed human survival, depends upon our understanding and judgement of that which is not human.

Gilgamesh has all the appearance of a human, indeed superhuman, but he is part god and so not human. His behaviour is autocratic, his actions following the ego driven needs of a two year old. His power, and how he uses it, creates a distance between his self and the people, and it is only through violence that he is able to connect with Enkidu. As the story progresses he continues to bend the world to his will, ultimately causing the death, and so loss, of that which sustained him. In order to begin to learn what it is to be human he faces his own death.

Just as with *Gilgamesh*, the scheme of work *Prometheus* encourages the class to take a stance – to 'see things rightly', as Plato has it. The work juxtaposes events and decisions so that the class can explore from whose point of view Prometheus' punishment is just. Here the adolescents' growing ability to sort out their subjectivity – to know and realise that they have a subjective point of view, that others will not necessarily see things as they do, is being woven into the fiction. If Prometheus hadn't stolen the fire would we (us humans) be where we are now – for good or bad? Would we be facing melting polar ice, and the threats brought about by the international arms trade if Prometheus had not stolen fire and given it to the humans? Was it a crime? Which aspect of it was a crime – theft or gift? Should it be punished?

Punishment a hot issue in school, and children argue for terrible punishments when in role as gods. We have to put the punishment in the context of the completed action that has been taken and seek to see revenge for what it is. Prometheus did what he did – knowledge exists, people are able to manipulate the material world in a highly sophisticated way, arrange things at sub-atomic levels, see what cannot be seen, put matter to use.

When I worked on Prometheus following the destruction of the World Trade Center in New York in 2001, the children were like Geiger counters – you could almost hear the anxious little clicks registering a high level of disturbance, see it in their movements, hear it in their vocal register. This scheme of work allowed them to give voice to what they need to know and say about inhumanness. At the time of writing, it still does.

My present year seven class told me that what the people need are weapons, particularly guns. They live in an area where gun crime is an issue – some of the students in our school have had their family members shot.

■ A story that has stood the test of time – past, present and possible

The right story can allow teachers to fashion learning zones that enable students to create the work as it unfolds and so learn to organise for future behaviour. As Alex Kozulin (1998, p151) says, 'students should be capable of approaching problems that do not yet exist at the moment of his or her learning'.

By participating in an unfolding, collaborative discourse, within in a set of carefully chosen givens, the class are learning through and about the creation of culture, of meaning. By living through a story set in the past, for example, as it unfolds in the present, the participants are engaged in predicting and making that which happens next.

Gilgamesh has the potential of a double past context, which places it in the sphere of the possible. It was written 3000 years ago so is set in ancient times. It was pulled from beneath the sands of time 150 years ago by an explorer, having long vanished from human knowledge,

and so is something that has to be discovered – it has possibility. As the teacher pulls the text from beneath the sands of time, she means to mediate the students' understanding of time and place.

In *Prometheus*, as the class work in small groups on how the people lived before they had fire, they are also learning how to work in a group now. The teacher can watch and coach on the interdependency of the group and the social skills that lead to survival.

With *The Cooks*, the denouement is presented through a sudden leap forward in time, and the participants have to consider the reported actions of the characters from a new distance, organising their behaviour from a double perspective.

■ *Normativity*

The fiction allows the class and the teacher to enter into, and live through, the same world. In classroom drama it can afford particular insights.

The fictional world has to be a world that is substantial enough to be credible, be bound by material considerations, and at the same time be flexible enough for reference to the differing experiences and knowledge of the participants.

For example, in *The Cooks*, the activity of the cooks must refer believably to the processes of food production, yet the menu must be broad enough to allow the class to choose familiar foods with which they can become experts.

These three lengths of yarn: the culture of the fictional world, the substance of the material world and the reference to the world outside, are woven together with a fourth, that of the stance of those involved, to form a mutual cultural landscape that should hold us in relation to each other so that we can explore how one ought to be. What will these cooks, in this kitchen, cooking this food for this King, do when facing the dilemmas the story presents them? And it is not just in the fiction that we are discovering how one ought to be – in the very doing of this classroom drama we are also finding out how, despite our seeming differences, humans can know what it is to be human, and step into a shared world.

In *Gilgamesh* the epic form allows us to pursue this further. Each turn of events contains a consequence of the previous actions, yet the episodes can stand in contradiction to each other. King Gilgamesh is cruel and greedy; the people seek justice from the gods. Enkidu releases the animals; the trapper seeks justice from Gilgamesh. Thus there is a contradiction in the people's understanding of where to seek justice, and the characters in the story do not live in exactly the same world. The material conditions of the gardens are bound by climate, soil, and knowledge, but the gardeners and the king live in them differently. How one ought to be becomes a matter of, as Michael Rosen (2004, p25) puts it, the 'social and ideological outlooks'. It is also a matter of power.

■ A meaning that lends itself to being opened out in relation to the material world

As I create SoWs, I fashion them, simply, around dramatic structure, and search for the concrete objects in the story.

Dramatic structure	Scheme of work	Commentary
Context – prologue and exposition	The cooks set up their kitchen and their expertise. They make meals for the king and his armies	Time is invested in the exposition to establish a language with which to explore the normative parallels. Contained within the normalcy are all the seeds of that which is to follow. The material circumstances place them so. The paper artefacts are symbolic mediators for the matter of the actions
Development – action and reaction	The new queen arrives; they make meals for her, then her son	This context and framing of the drama allows for a collective witnessing of the unfolding of events and actions – it encourages the distribution of intelligence. The distance of this frame is both near and far – the kitchen is removed from the royal rooms – the cooks do not mix with royalty, although they may be familiar with them – they witness and are at times privy to intimate details of the life of their 'masters' but they are essentially a servant class, but a (royal) child may go into a kitchen, as may a new queen. also the cooks create the meals that the royals put inside themselves each day and their job of work is at the very centre of the most horrifying aspect of the story – cooking and serving up a child as a meal
		Thus the collective frame must be strong enough to carry the contradictions – it's not about the differing views of various characters but what happens as the differing views form a distributed intelligence
Crisis/climax	They find the hidden, damaged Philomel. They feed her too. They pass a message from her to the queen	The key events of the story are a given, the heroes actions are a given – what we address are the social implications for and the actions of the witnesses – those whose hands carry out the work
Denouement – untying of knots	Move forward in time. The teacher recounts the crisis of the story the kitchen, disarranged. How did the cooks respond to the awful events and the desertion of the palace?	The story shifts in time – we are now in an uncertain future looking back at the crisis. Both form and content are disturbed and disturbing. The class should be able to hear these horrific acts from a safe distance. The reactions of the cooks to the awful actions of their masters. The particulars, to which Brecht's poem refers, are explored

Imagination in conference with experience

The teacher, holding the core principle at the centre, can thus bind the formal, the expressive-interpretive and the productive strands to form 'possible worlds that provide the landscape for thinking about the human condition' (Bruner, 1996, p154).

And in that bonding, a first rule of practice is suggested: the teacher must herself take an imaginative relationship to the story. She must ask questions of it. She must instigate a discourse between the story and her experience of what it is to be human. This may seem such an obvious thing to say, but it is a depressing fact that many teachers, alienated from their own practice by the demands made upon them by the government imposed National Curriculum and League Tables, are in danger of being satisfied by quick answers and systematised tick boxes. It is important that teachers, too, behave and feel like creative, expert, practising artists. Of course, they have to know a lot of other stuff. They must have a working knowledge of the class, individually and collectively, as well as of child development. Sometimes that can seem like a heavy load to carry in the daily press of school demands, but creating one's own relationship to the daily work we do is worth it. To get to know the story, to research its context, to give oneself a part in it, makes it live – and if it lives in the teacher, it will live better in the class.

The wellspring of a special way of teaching

Somewhere around 35,000 – 40,000 years ago humans began to paint on the walls of caves. Not clumsy daubs nor crude illustrations, these early expressions and impressions of the world are works of art. To stand inside the earth and fix one's eyes on these stone visions is revelatory – we have learned so much, and yet hardly anything at all, in the intervening millennia. Indeed, Picasso, on viewing the cave paintings at Lascaux, is reputed to have said *we have learnt nothing*.

I believe that it is not so much that we have learnt nothing, but rather that we, as a species, do not know what it is we know.

To those early artistic endeavours, through first philosophies and religions, across clay figures and massive stone structures, around centuries of development and change, classroom drama is connected. Strong strands form this connection to our common ancestry – art and understanding, imagination and reason. As it engages with the expression of human connection to the material world, with our interpretation of the meaning of matter and events, and the continuing formation of our culture, educational classroom drama is strengthening the bonds between these strands – bonds that go to the heart of what it is to be human.

We humans are a very young species which is why we are susceptible to pandemics – unlike, for example, lizards.

And like all young things, we need nurturing. We are, in a way, aware of this. Our reason informs us that the there are things we don't know about, and don't know how to do. The early Roman philosopher Lucretius put it thus:

> Our minds, disturbed by their inadequate knowledge of the truth are uncertain whether the world had a beginning, a birth and equally whether there is a limit to the ability of the world's wall to endure the strain of restless motion. (1969 trans, p101)

We have a concept of a lack, a gap, and we wad the gap with our imagination. This wadding can lead to strange conclusions and creations as, across the globe and ages, we search for answers.

Nevertheless, however diverse these answers may be, it is the case that the being of the human is materially and inescapably linked with the matter of the ever-changing planet earth.

Lucretius again:

> Both mind and soul are material.... the mind and the soul have a material nature. (*ibid*)

If he knew this then, we must know it now.

Around 350 million years ago the earth saw the biggest mass extinction of life. Eighty to ninety percent of all living things disappeared in the aftermath of huge volcanic eruptions. The survivors were a few small burrowing mammal-like reptiles. Move forward to 200 million years ago and now the dinosaurs dominate, whilst the first true mammals, small mouse-like creatures, are surviving by burrowing and living an insecure, nocturnal life. Another turn of the clock, and, 65 million years ago, another mass extinction takes place – sixty to seventy percent of all living things have gone out of existence. The reason why is still a matter of debate, but it saw off the dinosaurs and set the scene for the descendants of the mouse-like creatures, some of whom had ventured out of their burrows and were now scampering around in trees, to spend the next 65 million years turning into the humans.

It is a mere 100,000 years ago that homo sapiens began to establish itself, reaching Europe just 40, 000 years ago. Despite facing near extinction once or twice, six billion of us have, in a comparatively short time, come to dominate every quarter of the planet. This massive domination is the result of our developing physiology in combination with, and in response to, the matter that surrounds us. Our brains, our motor neurons are a coalescence of matter brought about by the changing world around us. And as our material being developed, so did our social/cultural existence. Painting in and on caves, creating figures out of clay and homes out of abris, are demonstrations of skilled, creative responses to experience and also manifestations of the formation of human culture – the two are completely connected.

The being of the human is fashioned, demonstrably, by the material circumstances as well as by the culture within which we live, at the same time as that culture and those circumstances are fashioned by their being. The two things are connected as matter of fact, as are all of us, one to the other – we share fifty-six percent of our DNA with a kiwi fruit, so how can it be that we humans are not deeply connected one to the other? Through our species' ancient and modern struggles for survival, our diversity has become a puzzle to us, and at times dominates our thinking. Each of us is unique -we have a unique DNA, and yet it is the DNA itself that binds us all, each to the other. It is that which helps us to understand and to see beyond the diverse expressions of what is different to the core of what is common – our humanity.

This world, material and cultural, whether we will it or not it, is in a constant process of formation and re-formation and we teachers, politicians, parents must know it, and help our young to *live* in it.

Section Two

Schemes for years 7, 8 and 9

Schemes for year 7

Prometheus

A scheme of work based on the ancient Greek myth of Prometheus

Introduction

This scheme of work was designed for year 7 and includes some notes on storytelling for the teacher. The background to its development is described in *Stating the Obvious*, as is its continuing development and progress.

The table below outlines links between this scheme and the connective curriculum described in the final section of the book

Content	Application and ownership of knowledge
	Application of technology
	Development of human knowledge
Concepts	Knowledge
	Technology
	Human need
	Progress of Human Culture – change
	Story
Skills	
Thinking	Developing story/plot
	Working through metaphor
	Structuring story – beginning, middle and end
	Reflecting on the work
	Asking questions
	Applying metaphor
	Working the matter (meaning and material)
Accessing knowledge and communicating understanding	Problem solving in a group. Working creatively with the class as a whole.
	Listening and responding creatively and socially in small and large groups.
	Developing creative work in a small group. Rehearsing. Participating in a presentation
	Working through metaphor. Taking on a mythic role
Physical and sensori-motor	Depiction into action
	Gesture of significant moments
	Movement to depict action
	Movement to express story
Learning Material	The myth of Prometheus
	Material content of everyday objects

Lesson 1: The Story

1. Circle, and introduction

The drama will be based on a story from Greek mythology. What do we already know about myths/Greek mythology?

Did the Greeks believe these stories?

2. Teacher tells class the story of Prometheus – as follows:

'Greek legends say that at the beginning of the world, long before humans existed, the earth was ruled over by gods known as the Titans. Their king, Cronus was wild and cruel. He was worried because he had been told that one day a child of his would kill him and take his place. To stop this from happening, Cronus swallowed all his sons and daughters whole as soon as they were born. Rhea, his wife, was very distressed by this. So when their sixth child was on the way she went to a cave secretly. She gave birth to a son. She hid him in this cave with some nymphs who would take care of him, and went back to Cronus. When Cronus found out that a son had been born, he was furious and went to look for him. To hide the baby well, the nymphs put him in a tree so that he was neither on the earth nor in the sky nor in the sea. They would make loud noises as Cronus passed so that he would not hear the baby crying.

Then Rhea took a large stone, wrapped it in baby's clothes, and gave it to Cronus as her son. He was fooled and swallowed it straight away. Now he thought he was safe.

The baby grew up into a fine lad. His name was Zeus. Rhea went to Metis, a wise Titaness, to ask for advice. Metis gave Rhea a plan to overthrow Cronus. Rhea brought Zeus to Cronus as his new Cup-Bearer (to taste and serve his wine). Cronus, who did not know this was his son, soon started to trust Zeus greatly.

Then one day, Zeus mixed a potion and poured it into his father's wine. The potion made Cronus violently sick, and out of his mouth came his other children. They were unharmed and wanted revenge. The two other sons, Hades and Poseidon, persuaded Zeus to start a war against Cronus and his followers'.

3. Pause for discussion if needed.

The story continues:

'This war was long and bitter. At last the three brothers went to ask for help from the one-eyed Cyclops who were in Cronus' prison. They freed them and in return the Cyclops gave them presents: to Hades a helmet that would make him invisible when he wore it; to Poseidon a three-pronged trident; and to Zeus a thunderbolt. The three brothers found Cronus alone.

Hades, wearing his helmet, stole Cronus' weapons.

Poseidon threatened him with his trident. Zeus crept up behind and struck him, with his thunderbolt. Cronus was instantly killed. The war was won.'

'Once the war against Cronus was over. Zeus turned his thoughts to love. He decided that the beautiful Metis, who helped him overthrow his father, should become his wife.

Notes

Before the lesson:

Have key words ready for display.

Do we need to believe stories to learn from them? Why is it helpful to 'suspend disbelief' when working with stories?

Teacher uses story-telling skills; e.g. use of pause, eye contact, emphasis, and levels.

Lesson 1: The Story (continued)

'Metis did not want to marry Zeus so she turned herself into a fish to escape him. He too became a fish, and swam after her. Then Metis leaped from the water into the air. She turned into an eagle and flew away from Zeus. He became an eagle too and flew after her. There was no escape. Metis gave up and married Zeus.

When Metis became pregnant, Zeus went to the oracle at Delphi. He asked it to look into the future and tell him if the baby would be a boy or a girl. The oracle said

'Oh mighty Zeus. The first-born child of Metis will be a girl of many gifts, talented, wise, and good. But beware: if Metis has a second child, it will be a son who will overthrow you, just as you overthrew your father, the once all-powerful Cronus.'

Zeus was not happy about this at all. He decided he would take no risks, even with the first child. He swallowed Metis whole before the baby was born.

Zeus then got a terrible headache. He could not get rid of it. He sent urgent word to another god, Hephaestus, to help him. They decided that there was a spirit inside Zeus which had to be set free. So Hephaestus drove a wedge into Zeus's head so the spirit could escape. It was not a spirit who came out though; it was a beautiful young girl. Zeus knew that this was his daughter, Metis' child. He called her Athene and she was the goddess of wisdom.

Now, Athene had a friend – a Titan called Prometheus who had helped Zeus in the war to defeat his father, Cronus.

It was Prometheus who made the first men out of clay. Resting one day by the river he was playing with the clay on the bank. He noticed that the shapes he made were not unlike the gods. He shaped them to walk upright. Prometheus made them and Zeus, king of the gods, breathed life into them'.

Lesson 2: Story into Action – The Breath of Life

Notes

Modelling possibilities

1. In centre of circle:
    – 1 pupil = Prometheus
    – 1 pupil = Zeus
    – 1 pupil = clay

    Depiction – 'Prometheus moulds the clay into a human being for the first time'.

    Teacher questions:
    ■ What position tells us they're human and not clay?
    ■ How can we see what the relationship is between Zeus and Prometheus?
    ■ What movement will signify Zeus giving the breath of life?
    ■ At what point does clay become human? How can we tell?

2. In groups of three, rehearse the moment when clay becomes human. Remind the groups of the questions above.

3. As each group present their scene the teacher again places the questions.

Challenge and develop the possibilities modelled above.

Lesson 3: What human beings need

1. Circle – teacher begins;

   'So, the first people are walking the earth – what is life like for them?'

2. Teacher narrates the continuation of the story:

   'These first men and women were still primitive beings. They lived by eating the animals they could kill with their wooden bows, horn axes and knives, and ate the few plants they knew how to gather. These first people did not know about fire, so all their food was eaten raw and they wrapped themselves in thick furs to keep out the cold of winter. Without fire to make ovens they could not harden the clay, nor could they work with metal. So they could not make bowls or jars to store things in, nor could they make good tools or weapons.'

3. In small groups – 3 depictions:

   What life was like for the men and women at first.

   ■ *Finding food*

   What type of food have they found?

   How are they eating it?

   ■ *Night-time*

   Where would they sleep?

   How would they protect themselves?

   ■ *In winter*

   What would it be like?

   How would they survive?

   How would they keep warm?

4. Spotlight moments from the work of the groups.

5. Whole class discussion around the questions

   What things would make life better for these people?

   What do they need to know?

   Teacher records the responses.

   Keep the focus on what human beings actually *need* in order to live a safe, healthy, fulfilled, social, happy life.

6. Teacher narrates:

   'The life of these people was very hard indeed. Prometheus saw their hardship. Prometheus told Zeus

   'They must be taught the secret of making fire, otherwise they are as helpless as children. We must finish what we have begun.'

   But Zeus was firm. He replied

   'They are content with what they have. They don't know any better, so why worry about them?'

7. Inside a circle, two pupils depict Zeus and Prometheus. Discussion around – What is the relationship between them now, in contrast to before? Why is this? Why is fire so important to each of them?

Lesson 4: The Getting of Fire

Before lesson set up 'fire'[hidden if possible).

1. Circle discussion: What things do we have in our lives that do not depend on fire (heat) for their manufacture?

2. Teacher reveals 'fire' and tells the class:

   'The fire on Mount Olympus is kept in a sacred place. The guardians of the fire guard it. Yet this did not deter Prometheus from stealing it'.

   Discuss who or what guards the fire.

3. Small groups: a freeze showing the guardians of the fire.... bring to life for 1 0 seconds,
   - What is the quality of their movement?
   - Do they move in unison or separately?

   Repeat and rehearse, with teacher coaching the quality of the movement and spotlighting.

4. Small groups continue and prepare five depictions showing how Prometheus steals the fire. What is the quality of the way in which he succeeds?

   As the groups show their work Teacher helps the class to focus on the question above.

5. Circle discussion/summary: Teacher asks 'what do the people have now that Prometheus has given them fire?'

Notes

I use a bundle of crepe paper and sticks or nightlights/candles depending on the class and the situation

This discussion can be exciting and challenging. In most classrooms there are very few things that haven't been manufactured without heat being used during some part of the process.

How is power/ knowledge guarded (made inaccessible) in our society?

What can be brought out in the quality of the movement?

These depictions can be developed into a piece of structured movement, sequenced to music.

Lesson 5: The gods retaliate – what will the people do?

Notes

1. Circle. Tir as Zeus calls a meeting of the gods. Pupils introduce themselves as particular gods around the circle.

2. Class in role discuss if Prometheus should be punished, and if so, how. Whatever the gods say, Zeus will decide that Prometheus should be tied to a rock and have his liver pecked out every day by an eagle.

   Class in role freeze at end of meeting as Zeus dismisses them. Teacher (out of role) feeds back what she can see on the frozen faces of the gods.

3. Small group depictions: how do the *people* react when they hear of Prometheus' punishment? Let's listen in to what some of them are saying.

   Spotlight.

4. In the same groups: make a plan for what the people do about Prometheus … each group reports back on, or shows, their plan.

5. It might be that the class would like to work on carrying out the plan – the teacher needs to judge whether they need to or not – this could be improvised in circle, with teacher or pupils telling it as the closing moments of an old myth being told around the fire.

6. Key question in circle:

   If Prometheus were here now, what would he steal for us?

   Explaining question – what do humans need now?

   Supplementary questions:

   ■ Where is the fire now?

   ■ Is it still under guard?

7. Small group depictions – What would Prometheus give to the human race now?

This section could be extended if the teacher thinks it would benefit the class to work in role as gods, creating the ethos of Mount Olympus, or taking on 'godly' personas. This can be an opportunity for members of the class to play those they are in conflict with or fear.

This can be refined depending on what's going on in the world and what the class needs.

Stating the Obvious

A workshop for teachers based on the Prometheus scheme of work

What follows is the transcript, more or less, of a session for drama teachers, which I conducted as part of a day's conference organised by the National Association for the Teaching of Drama (NATD), following the events of September 11 2001.

Additional comments (in boxes) have been added in the writing up of the session, to make it more transparent to the reader.

The Teaching Problem

How do we go about teaching authentically in the midst of a massive disturbance? One that implicates both the children and ourselves.

What follows is offered as a pattern for possible classroom practice. It rests deliberately and carefully on the opportunities offered by the creative fiction. It enables the teacher to develop the opportunities that are seized by the class.

It is not a story about war. It is a story about knowledge and human development. It is about our past, and so it is also about our future.

Part One

I'd like to begin with two short anecdotes.

The first is taken from a description of a moment during a lesson at the time of the Gulf War in 1991. Then too America and Britain had set an ersatz deadline. The *day* referred to is the day after the deadline.

1. That day one of the fourth years asked me if I had attended the peace march the previous Saturday, organised in protest against the likely eventuality of war. When I told him that I had not, he asked why. I explained that I had been at a meeting discussing a conference for drama teachers on the war.

> 'Oh' he said, and wandered back to his group. A minute later he reappeared.
>
> 'Yes, but what are you going to *do*?'

2. Three weeks before this conference I was talking to some of my former 6th formers. They had come to visit, for a chat. We talked about the war and the events of September 11th 2001. One of them, who was just about to embark upon a course in which she would train to be a drama teacher, said

> 'I didn't really take it all in at first. It was all in black and white – wasn't it? – until I saw a colour picture in the paper the next day of a little girl who was on the plane. When I saw that I thought 'what would you say'? If I was her mum, *how* could I tell her what was happening? And then I really cried.'

I'm sure we all have similar stories to tell. Writing them down can focus our thinking and sharpen our reflective practice.

So what do we *do*? *How* do we tell children what is going on?

What can we *do*?

It seems obvious to me that what we do is provide classroom Drama.

Although we adults also need to explore and understand our feelings and reactions, we can't wait until we've sorted them out before we get on with it in the classroom. We (us and the children) do not have that kind of time. We'll miss the moment. Of course many of us are nervous of dealing with such painful and far-reaching issues, but the children need our work now. It is now that they are afraid, and vulnerable to oppressive ideas.

What we drama practitioners know about is

- drama
- teaching children.

It is up to us to provide children with a safe, child-centred, creative, and social forum, or better still, a crucible in which these massive disturbances of matter and mind can be synthesised.

It may be useful to address this concretely.

> The assertions above are central to the practice of a humanising curriculum. Many teachers and educators did in fact miss the moment. More than that, they advocated missing the moment. A child's life, as well as the historical development of the human race, is a connecting spiral of such moments. What price do we pay if we miss them?

How do we help children understand what is happening?

What follows is a description of work in progress.

What you can do is plan where this work should go next.

There are certain schemes of work that I come back to again and again. I had forgotten just how long I'd been doing this particular scheme of work until I re-read the article in *Theatre and Education Journal*.

I originally developed this scheme of work from a Theatre in Education programme by Actors' Group. It centres on the myth of Prometheus.

I have found the mythic (*possible explanation the workings of the universe, nature and human history*) and allegorical (*use of symbolic fictional characters to illustrate the world*) qualities of this old story provide an excellent mortar for the work of our classroom crucible. I have been working on this scheme with a year seven class. This is where we've got to so far.

Brief Outline of Prometheus
Scheme of Work (so far)

1. Teacher tells the story of Cronus swallowing his children, the hiding of Zeus, and the overthrow of Cronus by his sons, including the Titan Prometheus who helped Zeus in his battle against his father. This part of the story concludes as Prometheus fashions clay figures.

2. Pair work – Prometheus and clay. Prometheus asks Zeus to bring the clay figures to life. How did the clay transform from matter to mind? Focus on quality of movement and facial expression. What were the first words spoken by human beings?

3. Groups – three depictions – what was life like for these first people? They didn't have fire.

4. Discussion – is there anything in this room that doesn't owe its genesis to the discovery of fire? This can be quite a lengthy and fascinating discussion involving physics and manufacturing processes!

5. Groups – movement/mime – how is the fire guarded? How does Prometheus steal it? Use music as a stimulus and a constraint.

Four key questions arise, and I note the answers given by one year seven class. The first two are questions that are normally asked in this scheme:

1. What did fire bring that helps us to be human?
2. What did fire bring that stops us from being human?

The answers the class gave to the first question were: *cooking, sitting around it together, light and warmth, and vacuum cleaners.*

The answers to the second were: *guns, bombs, terrorist attacks, arson.*

The two other questions I added this time were:

3. Is there anyone living today who might regret that humans ever discovered fire?

4. If Zeus and Prometheus could see how we are using fire now what would they do?

Questions 3 and 4 are an example of how the teachers can develop the opportunities that are seized by the class. Their answers to questions 1 and 2 guided me to the next questions I should ask. Note that not once did I mention war.

When I asked question 3, I was aiming to sharpen the focus for question 2.

Question 4 brought these responses:

Zeus would be pleased – we shouldn't have had fire in the first place – it serves us right

Zeus would let the war go on to teach them a lesson

Zeus would let the war go on and then take fire back

Zeus would take the fire away and blame Prometheus

Zeus would be happy at the attacks because Prometheus stole it and so it's a punishment

Zeus would kill Prometheus and take the fire back

Zeus would chuck Bin Laden in prison

Zeus would kill Bin Laden and help the people of Afghanistan to build their houses and punish those who were in with Bin Laden

Zeus would kill Prometheus and then give people another chance with the fire but tell them they only have one more chance with it

Zeus realises it would be hard for people to do without the fire as they have had it for so long

Zeus would help the people in the US and Afghanistan and take away the guns and punish Bin Laden

Prometheus would take the fire back and give it to the gods.

Where would you take this work now?

Start by looking at the responses:

Do they fall into any particular categories, and if so what they tell us about the needs of the class?

What disturbances do they trigger in you as a classroom teacher?

How can you manage the work so that all the children in your class feel valued?

What brotherhoods might we be in?

What would you ask the class to do next?

The session ended as the teachers began to plan the next stage.

The Prometheus Scheme of Work continues to be used in school and beyond.

In 2004 it provided a starting point for *The Prometheus Project*, a joint venture between the Gjilani Youth Theatre from Kosova, and the Dukes Youth Theatre in Lancaster.

I am indebted to the late Tony Grady for his helpful comments during the writing of this piece, and for giving me the title.

The Song

A scheme of work based on the actions of Harriet Tubman and the conditions in which she lived

Introduction

This scheme of work began life as a year 8 scheme, and is currently taught to year 7. It was born out of a combined History and Drama project that I devised for Black History Month, a regular event promoted in schools in order to recognise and celebrate the achievements and contributions of black people in the world.

Just recently one of my year 12 students said 'I wish we could do Harriet Tubman again – I really liked that story'.

I quizzed him on what it was about the story that he liked. He wasn't sure – he said – 'She escaped – I looked forward to those lessons'.

There is also an excellent scheme of work on Harriet Tubman by Jon Airs and Chris Ball, *A Cross Curricular Drama.*[1]

I would like to acknowledge the work of Maria Blanco who worked alongside me on this scheme of work during her PGCE year.

Content	Slavery
	Resisting inhuman acts
	Retaining humanity
	Social nature of survival
Concepts	Oppression/freedom
	Collusion
	Humanity/inhumanity
Skills	
Thinking	Problem solving in large and small groups
	Responding thoughtfully to others
	Responding to stimuli and developing the drama
	Predicting
	Seeing wider implications
	Use of symbol
Accessing knowledge and communicating understanding	Establishing space (imaginatively) and place
	Creating a role
	Conveying messages

Accessing knowledge and communicating understanding (continued)	Listening for understanding Re-phrasing, questioning for understanding, indicating key words Dramatic action Reporting Depiction Thought tracking Writing in role Connected narrative Sound, silence and song
Physical and sensori-motor	Establishing space (imaginatively) and place. Adopting and sustaining a role, (showing attitudes).
Learning Material	The actions of Harriet Tubman American history. Black history.

Lesson 1: What is a slave?

Notes

1. As the class enters, the song *Harriet Tubman* is playing.
   When class is settled Teacher plays the track again, with extract from song written on the board.

2. Circle. Teacher asks the class to discuss the words to the song and inform the class that Harriet Tubman was a slave in America. She was born into slavery in Maryland, America, in about 1820. At the age of five or six, she began to work as a house servant and seven years later she was sent to work in the fields.

3. Teacher asks for volunteers to create a class sculpture in the middle of the circle entitled 'slavery', using the definition to help focus the work.

4. Teacher talk – 'While she was still in her early teens she saw an angry overseer turning on another field hand. She tried to protect him and was hit on the head with a heavy weight. She never fully recovered from the blow and often wore a headscarf to hide the scar. One day, fearing that she or her sisters on the plantation would be sold, Harriet escaped and made her way to Pennsylvania and soon after to Philadelphia, where she found work and saved her money. I wonder why she stayed so long and what finally pushed her to escape'.

5. Teacher organises a small group depiction-action-depiction entitled 'the last straw'– an event that pushes a slave to finally risk trying to escape. The groups show their work.

6. Teacher talk – 'For more than a decade Harriet made numerous trips back to the South to bring slaves to freedom in the North. She armed herself with a rifle and devised clever techniques that helped make her journeys successful. By 1856, Tubman's capture would have brought a $40,000 reward. She became known as 'Moses'. John Brown, a famous abolitionist, once said she was *'one of the bravest persons on this continent'*.'

   Next lesson we will see how she led slaves to freedom.

Notes column:

Harriet Tubman by Holly Near and Ronnie Gilbert – a song.

Have ready for display –
– words of song
– definition of a slave (see resources)
– world map

Indicate Maryland on world map

Lesson 2: Music to free people

1. Teacher talk; 'Song was a key way of passing information. The night before she was going to lead an escape Harriet would walk past the slave quarters in the dark and sing an old spiritual about Moses leading the slaves the freedom. That was the signal to get ready to leave.

   Few slaves could read or write, and slaves passed on maps for escape routes to each other through song. We're going to learn part of a slave map song.'

   Teacher teaches class a verse or two of the song.

2. Teacher organises the class into small groups to create
   - an escape or map song/verse
   - a scene in which the song is passed from one field hand to another without the overseer realising what is going on.

   The groups show their scenes, including the songs/verses. Teacher gives feedback on the tensions at work and the 'map'.

Notes

I learnt this song as a young teenager. If you are not able to find out the tune, then use it as verse

The pupils usually enjoy this. Teach this a line at a time, building one upon the other. If possible, avoid writing it down for the class, thus encouraging them to learn orally/aurally

Encourage the pupils to build their songs/verses together line by line, verbally. Encourage them to learn orally/aurally

Lesson 3: The Underground Railroad

Notes

1. Teacher talk; 'It wasn't just the songs that used codes. Harriet Tubman created the 'underground railroad' which was neither a railroad nor underground. It was code for an escape route for slaves escaping from the south to the north. There were 'conductors', such as Harriet, 'stations', which were safe houses, and 'parcels', which were the slaves. The whole thing was very high risk'.

2. Circle. Teacher asks class to discuss in pairs – 'what would happen if
   - a conductor was caught
   - a station master was caught
   - how might the penalties differ for black people and white?'
   Report back to circle.

   Pay attention to class dynamics, and strengths and weaknesses when casting pupils to play the characters of slaves.

3. Teacher creates a scene in middle of circle – one student or teacher in role as Harriet is persuading another in role as a 'free' person (e.g. a farmer, or someone who has a place of business) to let their home/place of work be used as a UGR (Underground Railroad) 'station'(safe house). What's at risk?

   As the scene progresses Teacher asks the class to evaluate the tensions at work here.

   What choices does this dilemma present to the people who are 'free'? What have they got to lose?

4. Teacher organises the class into small groups and allocates each group, except for one, a 'station' e.g. a family run farm, a blacksmith's shop, a graveyard, a funeral parlour, a schoolhouse.

   The 'station' groups are to develop a 30 second scene showing the characters who live/work at that 'station'.

   The other group are to represent a group of escaping field hands meeting for the first time as they travel on the 'underground

Lesson 3: The Underground Railroad (continued)

Notes

railroad'. They are to help each other demonstrate the feeling state of the field hands and the implications for action.

Each group demonstrates their work.

This demonstration can foreshadow the reason that Harriet carried a gun

5. Teacher allocates one of the pupils playing the field hands to one of the 'stations'. Teacher conducts small group spontaneous improvisations of the escaping field hands arriving simultaneously at their allocated 'stations'. Teacher lets it run for a few minutes then asks the escaping field hands to move on to the next 'station'. Teacher repeats this process, watching for increasing engagement and skill at demonstrating the key points. When she feels that the class are ready, teacher asks the field hands to move on one more time, this time showing each group's work one at a time.

Lesson 4: What Harriet Carries

Notes

1. Teacher talk: 'There were three things that Harriet Tubman carried with her on the 'underground railroad'– pepper, specially prepared syrup, and a gun'.

    Teacher places each object as she mentions it.

    Teacher asks the class if they have any suggestions as to why Harriet carried these things.

    Discussion.

    Teacher explains that – 'The pepper was sprinkled on the ground to throw the tracker dogs off the scent; the specially prepared syrup would make babies sleep so that they wouldn't cry and betray a hiding place; and the gun .... well let me demonstrate..........

    Have 3 objects ready that represent the objects that Harriet carries

    Listening for action

2. Teacher asks for volunteers to depict this in circle: 'The first, and according to history, and only time Harriet threatened an escapee with the gun'. Seven actors:
    - ■ Harriet
    - ■ the escapee
    - ■ Harriet's thoughts
    - ■ the escapee's thoughts
    - ■ one other escapee
    - ■ the other escapee's thoughts

    Teacher explains that Harriet and the escapees are travelling secretly at night. One of the escapees has become frightened and lost his nerve – he is scared and beginning to make a noise. Teacher asks the pupils who are watching why Harriet is pointing her gun at him. Teacher asks the pupils watching what the 'thoughts' should say?

    By asking the 'audience' to put in their ideas Teacher is protecting the pupils in the middle and keeping the focus on the different thoughts

3. Teacher organises the class into groups to develop the moment depicted in the circle. As the groups work, Teacher asks them to refine the work to demonstrate one key moment.

    Each group shows their key moment and Teacher asks class to give each key moment a title.

4. Teacher asks class to reflect individually and write what Harriet wrote in her diary that night.

    Teacher scribes the titles ready for the next lesson.

Lesson 5: Remembering

1. Teacher begins by asking class if they can remember the 3 things Harriet carried and what they were used for.

   Teacher refers to the previous lesson's key moments and shows the titles.

   Teacher says 'Harriet Tubman helped 300 slaves escape to Canada, all of whom survived their escape to freedom. I wonder how they all ended up – and their sons and their daughters, and their grandsons and their granddaughters.....I wonder what she would make of our world now – and I wonder what she hoped for the future'.

   Discussion.

2. Teacher says 'If we had a museum in honour of Harriet Tubman, what kinds of statues might there be in that museum?'

   Discussion. Teacher organises the class into groups, and asks them to create a sculpture of a statue or monument created in memory of Harriet Tubman. It should have some words carved on it somewhere.

   When all are ready the pupils inspect each other's statues.

3. Teacher asks – 'Is there anything else that we should put in place in order to remember the life and actions of Harriet Tubman?'

   As the class make suggestions Teacher organises them so that they can be realised and added to the museum.

   The class might, for example, suggest passing new laws, in which case a group might want to write out the laws, or they might want to draw pictures of events, or re-draft or record one of the songs.

   When all are ready each exhibit is demonstrated and scrutinised.

   Teacher rounds off 'You have remembered well'.

You could also ask one or two groups to show their key moment if appropriate.

The pupils could simply write on sugar paper and stick it to the statue, or they could cut the words out and arrange them around the statue.

Resources

Song – Harriet Tubman track 1 on *Lifeline* by
Holly Near and Ronnie Gilbert
Redwood Records

Definition

A slave is a person who

- is forced to work — through mental or physical threat
- is owned by an employer
- is bought and sold as property
- has little or no freedom of movement.

from http://www.antislavery.org/homepage/
antislavery/modern.htm

The Drinking Gourd

When the sun comes back and the first quail calls,
Follow the Drinking Gourd.
For the old man is waiting for to carry you to freedom,
If you follow the Drinking Gourd.

Quail are birds wintering in the south. The Drinking Gourd is the constellation of the Big Dipper. The old man is Peg Leg Joe. Leave in the winter and walk towards the Drinking Gourd. Meet a guide for the remainder of the trip.

The Ohio River is too wide and too swift to swim across. When the river was frozen escapees could walk across on the ice. It took about a year to travel from the South to the Ohio; slaves had to start their trip in winter in order to be at the Ohio the next winter.

The riverbank makes a very good road;
The dead trees show you the way,
Left foot, peg foot, travelling on
Follow the Drinking Gourd.

Follow the bank of the Tombighee River north looking for dead trees marked with drawings of a left foot and a peg foot.

The river ends between two hills,
Follow the Drinking Gourd.
There's another river on the other side,
Follow the Drinking Gourd.

At the end of the Tombighee, continue north over the hills until there is another river, then travel north along the new river, which is the Tennessee River.

Where the great big river meets the little river,
Follow the Drinking Gourd.
For the old man is waiting to carry you to freedom if you follow the Drinking Gourd.

The Tennessee joined another river. Cross that river (which is the Ohio River), and on the north bank, meet a guide from the Underground Railroad.

Peg foot = a slave who's tried escaping before and has had their right foot amputated

Schemes for year 8

The Cooks in the Kitchen

A scheme of work based on the ancient Greek myth of Philomel

Introduction

This scheme of work was designed for year 8, although it arose from work with 6th formers. We were studying Timberlake Wertenbaker's play '*The Love of a Nightingale*' as part of the 'A' level *Drama and Theatre Studies* course, and I became hooked by the 6th formers' reactions to the story. They were very taken by the events of the story as well as by the role of the women in it, and together we wondered why Wertenbaker omitted the section of the myth that tells of what becomes of Itys after he is killed. In her play he is given the last word – he says 'Didn't you want me to ask questions?' In the myth he is silenced most horribly. We explored this a little, and so the following scheme of work came into being.

This scheme of work offers an example of a whole class drama. It begins by establishing the context, and reaches beyond the time frame of the main story. It provides the pupils with a role that allows them to work at a safe distance from the actions of the main protagonists. At the same time it gives them the chance to get their hands on the (imagined) stuff or matter of the plot. Most of the work allows the class to work together in role, with the teacher moving between being in the drama and outside it. A sample front page outlines the content it addresses, as well as the concepts and skills it offers as possibilities for teaching.

The Myth of Philomel

There are two versions of this myth, the main difference being in the role reversal of the two sisters. The key events and actions remain the same. It is the story from which Shakespeare took ideas for his play *Titus Andronicus*.

There was once a king of the ancient state of Athens, named Pandion. He was father to four children two of them his daughters Procne and Philomel. And he was grand-father to Theseus... but that is another story.

King Pandion was at war, and needed help. He called on King Tereus, king of Thrace, who came and fought by his side to help him win the war. In gratitude King Pandion offered his daughter for Tereus to marry.

Now Philomel and Procne were close – they had grown up together, and although they realised that it was their royal duty to do what the king their father bid them, they knew they would miss each other.

Procne married Tereus and went back with him to Thrace. She was happy enough as queen of Thrace, and bore a son, Itys. She loved her son greatly, but missed her sister. Tereus said that he would bring Philomel on a visit , and he travelled to Athens to fetch her. On the return journey he attacked (raped) Philomel. To keep his outrage a secret, he cut out Philomel's tongue and hid her away in an isolated place. Tereus told Procne that her sister had died on the voyage.

Philomel wove her sad story onto a piece of needlework and sent it to her sister. Procne found Philomel and the two of them killed Itys, and served the cooked body of the child to Tereus. Tereus tried to slay the sisters as they ran from the palace. The women cried out for help from the gods and all three were transformed into birds: Tereus became a hoopoe (a bird with a crest who's nest has a foul stench) Procne a swallow and Philomel a nightingale.

Content	Economic human relationships Family relationships – responsibility Silenced expression Cause and effect
Concepts	What it is to be human Responsibility Nutrition
Skills: Thinking	Understanding cause and effect Responding thoughtfully to others Responding to stimuli and developing the drama Identifying sub-text Seeing wider implications Use of symbol
Accessing knowledge and communicating understanding	Negotiating relationships Problem solving in large and small groups Responding to stimuli and developing the drama. Establishing space (imaginatively) and place. Adopting and sustaining a role (showing attitudes). Conveying messages, giving instructions, connecting narrative. Sequencing scenes and structuring action Identifying sub-text Commenting on what has been said. Seeing wider implications
Physical and sensori-motor	Responding to stimuli and developing the drama Establishing space (imaginatively) and place Physicalising a role (showing attitudes)
Learning material	The myth of Philomel The unfolding of a family tragedy brought about by the consequences of war and the warrior stance, seen through the eyes of servants to the warrior

Lesson 1: The Cooks

1. Circle – Teacher talk:

    'Imagine a warm and sunny country...you can hear the cicadas in the evening and smell thyme (refer to dried herbs) when the sun is warm. Imagine a palace...the palace of King Tereus....imagine the kitchens...busy and noisy, producing wonderful aromatic dishes...where the best cooks in the land work, each with their own speciality. Imagine that you are one of those cooks; you are very skilled in cooking a particular food'.

    List on board...e.g.

    ■ pastry, deserts, cakes
    ■ meat
    ■ vegetable
    ■ fish
    ■ non-alcoholic drinks
    ■ farinaceous dishes
    ■ wines

2. Teacher encourages the class to discuss/negotiate chosen areas of expertise. (Tir as pot washer?) and to begin to set out the kitchen around the room. Each pupil establishes a particular station in the room – drawing their area (e.g. stove/fire, table of knives, herb cupboard) on sugar paper. These drawings should be retained for each lesson.

3. The teacher asks the class to prepare individual freezes to show as a whole class simultaneously. The freezes are to show three aspects of the work and then to be developed by running them together to form a mime. The teacher asks the class to show how the character's actions give a flavour of the feelings/mood in the kitchen as the cooks work.

4. The teacher moves the class from whole class simultaneous work to preparation of a 30 second scene with the person nearest to them in the kitchen showing everyday life in the kitchens.

5. As the class watches these pair scenes, teacher notes for the class what is being established about life in the kitchen.

6. Teacher then folds the work back into a whole class improvisation, using such structuring questions as 'who talks to who, who avoids who, who skives, who jokes, who is proud of their work, who bosses who?'

7. The teacher concludes by summing up the 'givens' that have been established.

Notes

Words on board with definitions of those you think the class might not know. You can use essential oils to help set the scene

Set out some kitchen objects on a table ... I used a white china bowl, dried herbs, a wooden spoon, dried mushrooms, an apron, a frying pan

I find that this talk of food is usually highly effective in drawing the class in. It triggers their personal preferences – they share likes and dislikes, their cultural experiences (note that some may carry unsafe feelings or memories)

NB if appropriate refer to Mediterranean foods such as honey, nuts, goat, sheep, fish, squid, flour, lentils.

The class are building a relationship to the many layers in the narrative, which are both then and now:

■ economic relationships
■ meals and their production
■ time and place
■ art form

Draw on the working relationships, the atmosphere – what the characters say to each other, what they do not say, what they convey through their body language.

Scribe

Some of these have been set by the teacher, some by the class

Lesson 2: The cooks prepare the soldiers for war

1. The teacher and the class re-establish the kitchens and the characters.

2. Teacher talk: 'Your king has bid you prepare a hearty meal for his soldiers. They are to march to war to help another king, King Pandion, the King of Athens. He is in trouble and has asked your King Tereus to help him.'

3. Teacher organises the class into small groups around sugar paper. Their task is to list/draw what the cooks will prepare for the hearty, sustaining meal, and perhaps the utensils they will use. The teacher and the class could take advantage of the opportunity for food education as the teacher goes around the groups.

4. Teacher asks the groups to report back and encourages the class to consider whether the meal is balanced/appropriate to the purpose.

5. Still in groups, teacher counts down to a freeze – 'preparing the food'. Move in to action – teacher interrupts with the following narration:

   'The situation has worsened – the King will have to send another battalion – more ingredients are needed quickly – the meat and fish cooks can't keep up – they select others to help them get more supplies of meat.'

6. The groups prepare 3 depictions:
   - Choosing which creature from the herd/flock/shoal.
   - Reaching for the creature.
   - Who kills the creature/how?

7. Teacher asks for depiction – 'back in the kitchen final touches are put to the hearty meal'. Teacher asks what the mood is in the kitchen? How can we tell? What is not being said'?

Teacher could do this in role as keeper of the royal provender

If the class do pursue this thread pay attention to:
- The relationship between social class and diet – differentiate between what the King eats and what is left over for the kitchen workers e.g. the meat for the king and the fat for the workers
- Consumerism and **food fashion** and packaging – the food that children have access to (e.g. pocket money, sweet shops, school dinners). Perhaps the keeper of the provender allows the kitchen staff to buy certain foods

This is probably a whole other scheme of work

Teacher could do this in role as keeper of the provender

This could pre-figure the meal that Procne later asks them to cook

Lesson 3: A New Cook Arrives

Notes

1. In circle teacher asks the class how the cooks spend their break times. e.g. 'Do they get break times? Lunch hours?'

2. Teacher counts down to whole class freeze – 'a new cook arrives from another state, Athens'.

3. Teacher brings whole class freeze to life – teacher-in-role as keeper of the provender or as pot washer (depending on which status would be appropriate to the class at this moment) and asks the cooks to help the new worker settle in, establishing in which area of food the new worker is skilled.

4. The class work in small groups devising scenes – what are they saying about the new worker? (How) do they help him/her settle in?

Or

Whole class role-play with teacher-in-role (Tir) as new worker.

The social being of the kitchen

Links with Refuge SoW

Testing the social

Some classes might need the kind of clear directions a higher status role could provide, whilst others will respond more effectively to the respectful suggestions made by a lower status character. Determining factors can include

- the teacher/class relationship
- the social health of the class
- the improvisational skills of the class
- the ability of the class to enter into the fiction
- what stage the class is at in their understanding of the content

This depends on whether the class is ready to sustain a whole class role-play.

Lesson 4: The Thing in the Shed

1. Teacher says 'The King was successful in the wars and returns with a new bride – Procne'.

2. Tir as the new queen Procne who has come to inspect the new kitchens – class in role as the cooks. She hopes they were kind to the new cook she brought with her. She misses her sister and her home. She is friendly, young.

3. Teacher continues with story.

   'Over time a child – Itys – is born. The cooks, especially the cake and pastry cooks, are pleased to have a child in the palace. Over the years they create the most sumptuous banquets, a christening feast, first birthday, 2nd birthday, 3rd, 4th, 5th. They become well known for creating wonderful parties, cakes in particular. The last cake was in the shape of a sword fit for a young Prince, and Itys was shaping up to be a fierce little warrior.

   Throughout all the feasting and happiness, however, the queen, Procne is sometimes sad. She misses her sister. The King sets off to bring her sister back. It is a long journey by boat, and on the way back he falls in love with the sister, Philomel. He tries to force himself on her. She resists but he wins, and afterwards, to keep her quiet, he cuts out her tongue.

   On his return, he tells Procne that Philomel died on the voyage. There are great lamentations and weeping. The cooks try to comfort the queen with special food and herbal teas. Gradually she is comforted, and time passes.

   During this time the cooks notice that the king's personal servant has been taking the scraps left over from the King's table to a crude hut at the far end of the palace grounds. No one is allowed near there. Until one day one of the cooks follows this servant to the hut and gets a glimpse inside. S/he sees a poor girl, wild and unkempt, making strange noises. S/he takes one or two of the others there later that day.'

4. Two or three pupils are asked to work in role, in the circle, as the cooks who have come to see the girl in the hut. Teacher-in-role as Philomel uses mime and gesture to tell the cooks of her plight.

5. Teacher narrates: 'Philomel gives the cooks a special cloth and asks them to take it to Procne. They do.'

6. In circle teacher-in-role as Procne, pupil as cook with cloth. Teacher-in-role demonstrates that the cloth is a tapestry telling her the story of what has happened – amazed and horrified, she thanks the cook.

7. Pupils speak one at a time around the circle – 'what can the cooks say now, and to whom?'

Notes

Have a cloth ready. It can be folded so the class isn't too concerned about what it looks like. Or use sugar paper

In role reflection on the previous lesson's work.

This isn't as difficult as it might sound. I have found that the pupils usually work it out quite quickly – especially if they were listening to the story you just told them! It's useful to wait until the class ask questions and keep the gestures simple and clear

Lesson 5: The Cooks' Choice

Notes

1. Teacher sets out objects in circle – some of the kitchen things are overturned and strewn in the centre, also a knife with a red cloth 'flowing' from it.

   Have the objects from lesson 1 ready in circle

2. Teacher describes the deserted palace: 'Everyone has deserted following a great calamity; each room lies empty and disturbed.'

3. Teacher asks the class what person might be the first to enter that deserted palace.

   Put the suggestions into categories (e.g. authority figure, ordinary person). Ask the class to choose a category and then choose one of the suggestions from that category (this is very quick)

4. Teacher asks for a volunteer to play that character and narrates this person exploring the palace, what they see etc. 'The last room they enter is the kitchen – they hear a noise in the scullery and go to investigate. What they see in the scullery is a young washing up servant scrubbing and scrubbing at an apparently immaculate pot.'

5. Teacher-in-role as pot washer driven to get pot clean. Pupil in role questions her, and Tir reveals the story:

   Of the murder of Itys – Of Procne's quiet seething as she entered the kitchen carrying meat (warm meat?) she instructed the cooks to cook – Of the unusual smell of that meat – Of the refusal of some cooks who gave up their jobs on the spot and left – Of some who followed orders – Of the cooking and serving of him to Tereus – Of the fury of Tereus when he discovered the nature of the ingredients and his chasing of Procne and Philomel from the palace – Of the servants absconding from the palace.

   If the pupil in role struggles with the questions, Teacher can come out of role and open up the questions to the class before going back into role, or ask them to suggest questions that s/he can ask. It may help to get pupil in role to look closely into the pot where s/he can see the ingrained specks of blood

6. Teacher out of role asks: 'how must it have been as the cooks left the palace?' and spotlights individual pupils asking 'what did your character drop or overturn or take with them as they left the palace?'

   To keep the tension of the story, quickly come of out role and ask the question with energy

7. Teacher asks for small group depictions showing three different moments 'as the cooks leave the palace'. The groups then select one for action.

8. The groups show and discuss the moments they have chosen. Teacher focuses the discussion on what the cooks did or did not say as they left the palace? Who did they say or not say it to?

   What the groups choose could well indicate a further lesson. This could demonstrate the class's understanding of the concepts and it may take more than one lesson for them to tackle this part of the story.

9. Teacher recounts the end of the myth, in which the three are turned into birds by the gods and denied human speech for ever.

   Teacher sets reflection task with the question 'who tells King Pandion what has become of his daughters and his grandson?'

Resources

Sugar paper, pens
Kitchen objects: e.g. a white china bowl, dried herbs, a wooden spoon, dried mushrooms, an apron, a frying pan.
Cloth to sign Philomel's tapestry.
Red cloth
Large pot

Refuge

A scheme of work exploring the experience of those of us who become refugees

Introduction
Starting Points

This scheme of work was a long time in the making – far too long.

The school I worked in when I wrote this scheme had around 980 pupils, about 180 of them refugees. A Refugee Co-ordinator was in post and regular weekly support from the LEA's Refugee Advisory Team. There was an effective induction programme for pupils who were refugees, as well as extra-curricular activities.

Even with such structures in place it is not always easy for teachers to find a way to approach refugee children in the classroom. There are many stumbling blocks, and questions the teachers might have often go unanswered because they are unasked. The important thing is that these children are children, who have need of teaching, just like any other child – but at times the stumbling blocks seem insurmountable in the daily press of classroom life.

It seems to me that there are three such blocks:

- The national curriculum does not make it easy for teachers to weave the life experiences of their pupils into the fabric of the daily classroom.

- The pressure and paperwork caused by the market forces operating suck up time and energy which could be spent on research, preparation and stretching or exercising our beleaguered imaginations.

- The anxiety of being inadequately prepared or informed, and perhaps provoking pain or distress in our pupils can cause us to hesitate, and sometimes stop altogether.

For myself the last block was the biggest. I came up with at least five different starting points over a period of almost two years. Each time I got no further than putting pen to paper.

Finally I re-discovered *The Peopling of London* and found I had a starting point I felt that I could trust.

Although this scheme of work is designed for year 8 pupils it can be adapted for other year groups and has been used with year 11 pupils.

It comprises mostly practical work and aims to demonstrate how the living experience of young people can be acknowledged within a protective fiction. It also pays particular attention to guided reflection.

It begins with the class examining case histories of people who have come to live in London over the past 500 years. From case histories they develop a profile of descendants living and working in London now.

As the scheme develops, it presents the class with an increasingly complex sequence of dilemmas arising from an internal conflict in an imaginary country. As the work progresses it can move between countries and roles, depending on the direction the drama takes.

The exact nature of the ending depends on the needs and work of the class.

I would like to thank John Wadmore and Elaine Evans for working alongside me on this scheme.

Lesson 1: Descendants

Notes

1. Teacher displays the time chart and asks the class to notice/discuss particular dates that might have significance or be topical.

   Resources: time chart, word list, case studies, list of freezes for display

2. Teacher indicates word 'descendant' and asks for/gives definition.

   Teacher shows example of case study and asks what this person's descendants might be doing now at home or work.

   The case study is a description of one individual who left their country and came to live in the UK

3. Teacher organises the class into small groups and gives each group a different case study. Teacher asks the groups to create a family living now that is descended from the person described in that case study, through three or four freezes showing aspects of the daily life of that family e g.

   - reading to the youngest/telling stories
   - cooking an evening meal
   - painting a room/putting up shelves
   - working in the garden
   - playing a game
   - washing clothes/cleaning shoes

   Be sure to show the real life of that family – keep it ordinary

4. The groups show (some of) the freezes. Teacher guides the class reflection on the freezes by asking 'What is life is like for them?' and gives a starting example of e.g. a bowl of cherries.

   Teacher asks 'If they all lived on the same street, what could we call that street?'

   Moving from the ordinary to the poetic. Guided reflection working metaphorically

   Usually the class, prompted by the previous exercise, come up with a name that is reflective of the content

5. The class return to their groups. The teacher gives a series of questions/instructions for the groups to work on:

   i) The family is getting ready for a welcome party for a new baby, a special family occasion – freeze showing the family gathered round the new baby.

   ii) One of the family remarks that the baby has great-grandmother's eyes – freeze.

   iii) Someone else goes to the family photograph album/box to check if this is true – freeze.

   iv) Devise a short scene in which the family look at the photograph album and find out what each of them has got from an ancestor.

6. The class shows the devised scenes – teacher guides class reflection with – 'What does this scene tell us about human history?'

Lesson 2: Refugees First

Notes

Resources: A4 poster saying REFUGEES FIRST, simulated newspaper extracts (see resources)

1. Some classes may need to be told that we will be working in role, and to remember the rules of working in role.

   Tir welcomes class to this emergency meeting of *Refugees First*:

   'A crisis has developed and we are the people who will have to deal with it. Before I begin to tell you about the crisis, it would help me to know just how much experience we have between us. I wonder if you could tell me how long you've been working with *Refugees First*, and whether your experience has been mostly here in the UK or in other countries.'

   Round the circle, all or some introduce themselves.

   'As you know, civil war has broken out in Azim. The situation has been terrible for the people there, men, women, and children. Thankfully some of them are managing to get away. There is a plane loaded with refugees from Azim on the way and it's up to us prepare for their arrival.

   As experts we need to pool our knowledge on the crisis that has developed in Azim, so we can prepare as best we can in the time we have. If we don't get to grips with it now we may lose the opportunity to help people survive this crisis.'

2. The teacher brings the class out of role and places this reflection question: 'How can we help ourselves to be more expert on this crisis so that our drama can be truthful?'

   Discuss.

   In pairs, the class read one of the simulated newspaper extracts. The teacher asks them to highlight and then share information that might give us clues to what is going on.

3. Re-convene in role and share the knowledge about the situation that has been gleaned.

4. Tir: 'I know that we have here people who are experts on the culture of the Chovan Azimians. Who can tell us something about their culture?'*

   Class in role brainstorm on food, arts and traditions.

   Teacher-in-role guides the discussion to focus on what the needs of the refugees will therefore be and how best they can be prepared for.

5. In groups the class in role make preparations for the arrival of the Chovan refugees.**

6. Each group demonstrates what they have prepared and Tir inspects, reflecting back the quality of what they have done, e.g. 'I notice that this group has prepared a meal that will make this place a home from home' – 'I notice that this group has prepared beds that are as comforting as a bedtime story'.

* This section draws on the first hand knowledge and experience of class members, but offers them the protection of fictionalising it. Make sure it is respectful and realistic. It is possible that the tenor of this will draw upon the name the class gave the street in part one

** This should be discussed and agreed on by the class as a whole, with each group doing something different. If the social health of the class is poor, the teacher interventions/suggestions will need to be more visible. Some possible ideas are: information brochures with strong visual content; welcoming committee and speech; plans for dormitories; menu for first meal; plan of activities for children (NB: the form of these has usually been that of iconic representation).

Report back on the preparations that have been made.

Part 3: Dual Language

1. In circle – Teacher asks for a round in which each person says what they remember about the work so far, and what problems they have had to solve in and out of role (they could plan and report back in pairs).

   Teacher makes sure that the class remember that they have worked in role as

   ■ descendants
   ■ workers for *Refugees First*

2. Teacher asks class to spread out and get into pairs to show two freezes:

   – A *Refugees First* worker greeting one of the refugees as they arrive at the airport
   – Two refugees settling into the reception centre.

3. Circle – teacher-in-role

   'Welcome to this emergency meeting of *Refugees First*. Another plane full of refugees is about to arrive tomorrow. We didn't realise that there would be so many. We don't have any more space at the reception centre. What shall we do?'

   Class discusses. Tir 'remembers' that during the second world war, children were evacuated from cities to stay in the country, and suggests 'we could knock on the doors of people nearby and ask if they could have a refugee for a week until we sort something out.'

4. Teacher puts up the name of the street where the descendants live. In pairs the class improvise around the following scene:

   ■ A is one of the descendants;
   ■ B is one of the RF workers.
   ■ B does not know who A is. As far as B is concerned A is simply a householder.
   ■ A knocks on the door of B and asks if s/he'll take a refugee for a week, of course they'll get money for food etc.

   As the groups show their scenes the teacher guides reflection on the truthfulness of the scene – 'would it really be this hard/easy to find temporary homes for refugees? Why?'

Notes

Resources: visual cues for roles played so far
Reflection and evaluation

I have found it helps to have a visual cue for each role played so far – e.g. object, laminated word, perhaps the name of the street on which the descendants live

NB: not 'planefull' but 'plane full' – the former sounds disrespectful, the latter denotes quantity.

It might help to have this sequence written out on the board, or on cards.

I have included the third point as sometimes pupils are tempted to say e.g. 'well your grandmother was an immigrant – why don't you help out', which is not something the RF worker would know. Also it can short circuit the reflection that is to follow

There can be marked differences in the responses of children from differing backgrounds, depending on their investment. I have noticed, for example, that the most recently arrived sometimes choose characters that are the most ready to share whatever they have.

Part 3: Dual Language (continued)

Notes

5. In circle Teacher plus pupil (preferably one who speaks another language) demonstrate an improvisation showing a refugee arriving at one of the homes and settling into the descendant's house.

6. In pairs the class devise a scene as above. The scene must come to a conclusion. Teacher chooses pairs so that the pupils who have another language are 'shared out'.

   Teacher encourages the pupils to work in two languages.

This pupil can be prepared earlier in the lesson. It's useful if you reverse the roles – i.e. the descendant is not speaking English and teacher-in-role as a refugee is

NB: keep this improvisation short and without an ending so pupils have more chance to put in their own ideas when they come to do the scene (i.e. less teacher influenced)

7. Each group shows their (hopefully, dual language) scene.

8. Teacher poses reflective questions to be discussed in pairs and then reported back to the circle – ' What is the temperature of the way in which the refugee and the descendant interact with each other? How can we tell how they will get on?'

Be aware that the shift in the balance of status can provide a rich vein for humour. As pupils work in languages that others do not speak or understand it can give them a real sense of power and delight. I have watched scenes where one pupil speaks English and the other Kurdish, and all the Kurdish speaking children in the audience are laughing (with delight, not spite). I have asked them to re-run the scene with an interpreter allowing the rest of the class to share the humour. This has also given rise to demonstrations of the use of pause, comic timing, and the narrator/ interpreter's use of bathos.

Lesson 4: Outside Inside

Notes

1. Teacher asks pupils to spread out working individually around the room.

   Resources: paper and pens ready

   'In the spare room of descendant, the refugee is settling in. On the bed is your bundle, box, or bag. You begin to unpack the few objects you have brought with you. Where do you put them? What furniture is in the room?

   Some things you put away. Some you keep out. There is one item that you put very deliberately next to your bed.

   You sit on the bed and you remember some of the things you couldn't bring with you.

   Write them down.'

   Pupils write.

2. Teacher spotlight's some pupils – 'what have you
   - ■ put away
   - ■ kept out
   - ■ put by your bed
   - ■ left behind?'

   Teacher might ask some questions about the history of the objects.

3. In circle, teacher and class develop freezes showing what (else) the householder does to help make the refugee feel at home. Choose a name for the refugee character if there isn't already one (R).

   If you didn't get to the last exercise of lesson 3, do it now

4. Still in circle, Teacher says, 'R begins to settle in and feel at home a little. One day R comes into the spare room to find the householder holding one of their precious objects.' Freeze in centre. As the class looks at the freeze teacher asks for a round – each pupil says what one of the protagonists is thinking at this moment.

   Put some of those reflections on paper/board.

5. Teacher: 'I wonder how those thoughts got into their heads.' Discuss.

   Each pupil reflects. NB: It doesn't matter if pupils say the same things as each other during rounds. In fact, it is very likely that they will, as the class are all considering the same thing. The teacher will be able to recognise the quality of the repetition

6. In pairs, a freeze that comes to life for 30 seconds showing a moment that helps the class understand how one of those thoughts got into their heads. Place two chairs to represent the two protagonists.

7. The class watches one or two of the pair scenes and Teacher asks them to review the emotional journey of the refugee so far (e.g. leaving their country, arriving at Heathrow, arriving at the house) and asks 'what factors have influenced the behaviour of the protagonists?'

   This exercise explores an aspect of Heathcote's 'role' in her levels of explanation.

Lesson 5: The Agency

1. In circle, teacher asks for a round in which each person says what they remember about the work so far.

    Teacher makes sure that the class remember they have worked in role as

    ■ descendants
    ■ workers for *Refugees First*
    ■ newly arrived refugees

    Teacher talk: 'We will now be meeting some new characters in our story.'

2. Tir welcomes the class to the planning meeting and establishes that they all work for the agency as photographers – refers to past successes (the exhibition on the wall) and explains that they have been asked by *Refugees First* to do a similar campaign on the Azim crisis.

    Tir explains that they are the most experienced photographers in the agency and that the agency needs them to come up with some ideas. E.g. will they take the photographs here or in Azim or where? Tir notes the suggestions made by the class in role.

2. Teacher sets small group task – each group is to create 3 depictions showing the 'photographs' taken by the photographers. Each depiction should carry a title, which should be written. These 'photographs' are to be shown at the next meeting of the Agency.

3. When the groups are ready to show their depictions Tir begins the next meeting of the Agency. As the groups show back the 'photographs' Tir feeds back and questions the class in role, commenting and questioning on the effectiveness of their work and how it will help to raise money for *Refugees First*.

    'Now, we need to start getting some of these images put on to posters and out on to the streets! I wonder what people will make of them.'

4. Teacher asks the class to divide into small groups to prepare overheard conversations 'at the bus stop'. These conversations reveal how the public are responding to the posters.

    As the class listens to each of these conversations the teacher makes notes of what is said.

Notes

Resources: display of Amnesty International (see resources section) exhibition of photographs on classroom wall

During this introduction ensure that you talk about the form, so that they are enabled to be experts e.g. 'I remember you (to a particular pupil) took this photograph, I know I found it very moving, the way the children are grouped together, focused on the dirty water that they must drink. There are no adults in the picture – can you remember how you took it? Did the children know you were taking it? Did you talk to them? Was it a difficult photo to take?

If some are slow to respond ask them (still in role) to talk in pairs and then report back

This feedback and reflection focuses on the quality and nature of the group's demonstrated understanding of the subject matter and the framing of the humans within it. It connects to the teacher's talk about the form during exercise 2. For example, 'it is clear that this picture shows why these people had to leave their homes and country so quickly – I can see that you have put the people's faces at the centre of your picture – why is that?' or 'it is clear that these soldiers are pointing these guns at this family – I can see that you have put the gun at the centre of the picture and the people to one side – why is that?' or 'it is clear that these people are sitting on aeroplane with their faces turned to the side – I can see that you have sat the people very near to each other – why is that?'

These notes can inform the letters for the next lesson.

Part 6

Notes

1. Tir convenes an agency meeting again. 'Our poster campaign is certainly having an impact! There have been adverse comments about the campaign. It's too effective, upsetting. People say we should withdraw it.'

    Tir introduces comments from specific letters that have been written.

    Tir asks for the views of the class in role and discusses what course the Agency should take. As this discussion progresses Tir receives a memo from *Greenflash*. Tir reads this out to the class in role.

    Teacher-in-role asks the class what to do next.

Resources: letters criticising and supporting the campaign memo about *Greenflash* (see examples in resources)

The structure and planning of the rest of this lesson will depend on what the class suggests. The teacher has to create the ending anew each time in such a way as to bring together the learning points from the SoW, and that reflection will be planned for

Resources

The Peopling of London is a resource pack produced by the Museum of London. It contains case histories, interviews, images, a time-line, and a tape-recording – which catalogue and demonstrate the peopling of London from other lands, from the prehistory of the Thames Valley up until 1993, when it was published. This pack, and the book published alongside it, are now out of print. The only copy of the book I could locate belonged to a friend. The Museum of London has a few of the packs left, which it keeps for teacher workshops.

However, it may be possible for teachers/pupils to find their own case histories via their school's history department, a local museum, or their own school population. This research could be the starting point for the pupils' engagement with the work.

The *Azim* pack, a simulation exercise I found at the back of a cupboard, was produced by the ILEA in 1975, yet its basic premise remains disturbingly apt. It contains simulated documents cataloguing a civil war in the imaginary country of Azim. The thrust of the exercise is to enable 6th formers to try to avert, and then deal with, the crisis in Azim. For the purposes of 'Refuge' I used only the simulated newspaper extracts.

Your War, Our Lives! Protect Children's Rights are posters of photographs with text, produced by Amnesty International as part of their campaign to protect and promote children's rights.

Word List

family
generation
ancestor
descendant
Azim
crisis
refugee

Freezes you could do:

- cooking an evening meal
- painting a room or putting up shelves
- working in the garden
- playing a game
- washing clothes/cleaning shoes
- reading to the youngest/telling stories

The Letters

The 'letters' outlined below are schematic examples only. The actual content should be created by the teacher depending on

- the responses of the class in the 'at the bus stop' exercise
- the need for contradiction.

Dear Sir

Whilst standing at the bus stop with my family the other day I was shocked to see a very upsetting picture of some children in a war zone. I understand that these things really happen, but I don't think that we should have to see these images as we go about our daily lives – it's very disturbing.

Yours sincerely
M. Atkinson

Dear Agency

I am just writing a quick note to say that I was very moved by your powerful pictures. I for one will be making a donation to Refugees First. Keep up the good work.

S. Rennik

Dear Agency

Thank you so much for the poster campaign. It certainly has raised our profile. We have had several TV and radio interviews, and quite a lot of newspaper coverage. We are very pleased that we chose your agency to do the work for us. Your photographers really do understand the needs of the people we are working to help.

Heartfelt thanks
Refugees First

Dear Sir

You should leave world affairs in the hands of governments. These are political concerns and you will only make things worse if you involve yourselves. Make no mistake – I will be asking my MP to raise questions about this in Parliament.

Yours sincerely
G. Elliot

Dear Agency

We note with some concern that your recent poster campaign for Refugees First has put the situation in Azim in a very negative light. As you know, our company has several business interests in Azim, including our entire trainer industry. This negative publicity is having an unfortunate impact on our sales. We have been very pleased with the advertising work that you have done for us in the past, but we feel that if you do not withdraw from your work with Refugees First then we will have to withdraw our account from your agency. We do hope that it will not come to this.

Yours sincerely
David Brown
Managing Director
Greenflash

EKIOS TRUTH

Thursday, October 8.

STATE OF EMERGENCY IN AZIM

The Azim situation has become an international crisis. Azim's President, Dr. Sikiri, has taken over power, has dismissed the democratically elected parliament, and has become a dictator.

In a nationwide radio and television broadcast, President Sikiri announced a State of Emergency. He declared that he had suspended Parliament. He said he himself had passed the national budget which a few hours earlier had been defeated in the House of Representatives because of the opposition of the Chovan-Azimian Members.

President Sikiri announced that he had suspended parts of the Constitution dealing with personal liberty. He did not specify which articles of the Constitution he had suspended, except the right to be brought before a judge within 24 hours of being arrested. Police now have the power to detain people without trial if they are suspected of being terrorists.

In an attempt to justify his seizure of power, President Sikiri said the aim was to end violence between the Bayan-Azimian and the Chovan-Azimian communities. He did not mention the

LIBERTIES CURTAILED: CHOVAN-AZIMIANS APPEAL TO GENERAL JALUD

fact that the recent violence had been caused by the Bayan-Azimian extremist organisation, the Bayazims, which wants Azim united with Baya.

It was clear from President Sikiri's broadcast that there is no likelihood of an immediate return to democratic government. He promised to restore parliament as soon as violence has been ended, but he fixed no date for this. And, as it is a question which he himself would decide, his seizure of power may mark the beginning of a permanent dictatorship and the end of democratic rule in Azim.

Vice-President Kassim, the much respected leader of the Chovan-Azimian community, immediately denounced Sikiri's actions. Dr. Kassim described the State of Emergency as undemocratic and unconstitutional. He said it was a surrender to pressure from

Bayazim terrorists, and was designed to take away the rights and liberties of the Chovan-Azimians.

Vice-President Kassim also made the valid point that Sikiri had no power to tear up the Constitution, as it is guaranteed by an international treaty. He declared "I call upon the Government of Chov and other peace-loving countries to take immediate action to remedy the situation. We ask General Khalil Jalud to keep his warplanes and his army and his navy in readiness to defend the Chovan-Azimian community. We look to our Chovan motherland for protection for our way of life and our Chovan religion and culture."

However, Dr. Kassim said he preferred peace to war. He said "Rather than war, it would be better to divide Azim into two separate and independent nations, and so partition the island as we proposed in 1958. Meanwhile, I say to the Chovan-Azimian community that we are united in our fight for right and liberty; the constitution still exists; and I am still the Vice-President of Azim."

DARG DAILY NEWS

Darg, Thursday, 8 October

STATE OF EMERGENCY DECLARED: AZIMIAN PARLIAMENT SUSPENDED

SIKIRI ACTS TO AVERT CIVIL WAR IN AZIM

In a dramatic new development in Azim, President Sikiri has taken steps to halt the violence between the two communities in the island, and stop the drift towards civil war.

Making a radio and television broadcast last night, President Sikiri declared a State of Emergency. Certain articles of the Constitution are suspended. Police have been given the power to detain suspected terrorists without trial. Bayan-Azimian police have been reinforced on the line dividing the Chovan-Azimian quarter of Actark, the capital of Azim, from the Bayan-Azimian part of the city. It is in this area where most of the bloodshed during the past week has occurred.

President Sikiri has also suspended Parliament. He has, by emergency Presidential decree, passed the National Budget. This had been blocked in Parliament by the Chovan-Azimian minority, which they were entitled to do under the Constitution. The President said he was forced to pass the budget to save Azim from economic collapse.

President Sikiri promised to restore Parliamentary rule as soon as the violence had been ended. When law and order is restored new elections will be held and proposals made to reform the Constitution.

Strong protest by Chovan-Azimian leader

The leader of the Chovan-Azimian community, Vice-President Kassim, criticised President Sikiri's actions in the strongest possible terms. He described them as undemocratic and unconstitutional and a surrender to pressure from the Bayan-Azimian extremists — Bayazims — who want Azim united with Baya.

Vice-President Kassim alleged that President Sikiri was attempting to set himself up as a dictator.

The most serious aspect of Dr. Kassim's speech was what appeared to be an invitation to the Government of Chov to invade Azim to protect the Chovan-Azimians. Dr. Kassim is reported to have stated: "We ask General Khalil Jalud to keep his warplanes and his army and his navy in readiness to defend the Chovan-Azimian community. We look to our Chovan motherland for protection for our way of life and our Chovan religion and culture."

It was clear from Dr. Kassim's emotional language that the Azim affair is a time bomb which could explode into another Eutovian War. He frequently referred to the Treaty of Guarantee, which was signed by Danta, Chov, Baya and Azim at the Darg Conference in 1960, and which guaranteed the independence of Azim. He claimed that President Sikiri had violated this treaty, and Vice-President Kassim demanded international action to remedy the present situation.

PICTURE CARD 1

© Lord Mansfield 1993

The Peopling of London pack extracts from the Museum of London

PICTURE CARD 8
with interview extracts

HAJI MOHAMMED ABDUL RAHMAN'S STORY

Getting a job in Calcutta

'I joined my first ship at nineteen years old. My elder brothers were all seamen. On this ship, my cousin was the *serang*. I had lots of relatives on board too. I was British then. The *serang* was called Rohamali. I had to give him money to take me on. Before I went on this ship, I worked as a labourer to earn the money I needed.'

Life on board

'At that time you would have thirty or forty people sleeping in one room on bunks. It was very crowded. But I had many relatives on board and relations between the Asian sailors were friendly — very good.'

Working on board ship

'I was a coalman first, then a fireman, then an oilman. I was a coalman for eighteen months. My job was to take coal to the fireman to stoke up. It was incredibly hot down there.

We would go first to Australia then London or Bombay. The ships were meat ships with freezers carrying beef or mutton.'

Pay

'I worked in the engine room. It was very hot. I earned £36 a month doing shift work for eight hours a day. It was very hard work. We used to do the same work as the English crew but they got more money. If you were white, you got £40 a month, but any other race got £36.'

During the Second World War

'They needed people to go on the ships at that time because a British ship had been attacked and no one wanted to join. There was a shortage of workers because of the risk. So we were offered double money.'

'During the War a Lord of some sort came onto the ship and gave us all a silver medal for our work and courage. He told us to keep it safely and said: "after the war, you will get something back in return from us". But when the war was over, we never got anything.'

Settling in London

'I was a seaman for forty-two years. I came to settle here in 1965 because I was too old to get a job on ship again.

In my time I have been a religious student and a priest. I did Arabic studies. I did the Haj [Islamic pilgrimage to Mecca] in 1971, 1979 and 1981.

Before the War, I came to London many times. I had friends in Hessel Street. I remember that my first impressions were that it was snowy, foggy, freezing cold. There was no sun.'

© The Museum of London 1993

**Child collecting water from an open supply,
Gaza Strip, 1998.**
© Carlos Reyes-Manzo.

When people are forced from their homes
to live in refugee camps, children are
frequently denied access to basic services
such as clean water supplies, adequate
shelter or education. When conflicts are
unresolved, refugees can live in "camps"
for generations.

**Serbian children playing at war, Gorazde,
Bosnia-Herzegovina.**
© Dario Mitidieri.

Massive psychological damage is inflicted on
children caught up in wars. Children who are
subjected to or who witness violence may
suffer behavioural problems for years. This
damage is frequently compounded by
economic hardships caused by the death of
parents and displacement from their homes.

Schemes for year 9

Cassandra (The Priests)

A scheme of work based on the myth of Cassandra

Introduction

I initially created this scheme of work for year 9 students, and developed it for a workshop with teachers at the National Association of Teachers of Drama (NATD) conference in 2002.

As one of the workshop leaders in the run up to that conference, I was asked to read Edward Bond's *The Cap*. The notes in the teaching notes column reflect Edward Bond's work, which influenced my preparation.

The scheme was subsequently written up to include some of the thinking behind the work and commentary from two of the workshop participants. In this way a key element of whole class drama teaching is demonstrated, namely the manipulation by the teacher, in the moment-to-moment unfolding of the practice. For example –

- metaphor – e.g. the putting of the truths in an envelope
- teacher language – e.g. use of tense, the poetic, heightened story mode
- objects – real e.g. keys and imagined e.g. the door
- restricted choice – e.g. the temple areas
- moments of transition – e.g. going into the bath-house
- contrast of place – e.g. temple and bath-house
- class confidence – e.g. when a group is still cautious of one another
- silence and speech – e.g. what is said and what is not said
- stance inside and outside of the story – e.g. the treatment of a particular novice
- resonance – e.g. the use of song

I would like to thank Guy Williams for his generous and valued contributions to devising this scheme of work. I am also grateful to the late Tony Grady and to Margaret Higgins for their comments and reflections on the work as it unfolded.

The Myth of Cassandra

According to Homer's *Iliad*, Cassandra was daughter to Queen Hecuba and King Priam, the rulers of Troy during the Trojan War.

Cassandra was a beautiful girl, and Apollo, the god of many things, became infatuated with her. He gave her the gift of true prophecy, expecting more than gratitude in return. When Cassandra shunned the god he added a bitter twist to her gift.

He condemned her to tell the truth, but never to be believed. And so it was. Cassandra justly prophesied each twist of the unfolding story of the downfall of Troy, and at every turn she was disbelieved.

Her father, the king, did not know what to do with his disturbing daughter. He tried to keep Cassandra locked up and out of the way of the warriors of Troy lest she dishearten them.

When Troy finally fell to the Greek invaders, Cassandra was attacked and, some say, raped, by the Greek warrior Ajax.

When Agamemnon, the Greek hero, took Cassandra back to his homeland as his mistress she was killed by his vengeful wife, Clytaemnestra.

The goddess Athene eventually avenged Cassandra.

Lesson 1: What is a Myth?

1. What is a myth?

   Class discuss (briefly). Put suggestions on board. Then fill in from Wertenbaker's writing as needed:

   'What is a myth? The oblique image of an unwanted truth, reverberating through time. And yet, the first, the Greek meaning of myth, is simply what is delivered by word of mouth, a myth is speech, public speech. And myth also means the matter itself, the content of the speech. We might ask, has the content become increasingly unacceptable and therefore the speech more indirect? How has the meaning of myth been transformed from public speech to an unlikely story? It also meant counsel, command. Now it is a remote tale. Let that be, there is no content without its myth. Fathers and sons, rebellion, collaboration, the state, every fold and twist of passion, we have uttered them all... If you must think of anything, think of countries, silence, but we cannot rephrase it for you. If we could, why would we trouble to show you the myth?'

2. Teacher places questions, but does not ask for or accept answers
   - Do we have many or some unwanted truths in our world now?
   - Who knows these truths?
   - Do they tell these truths?

   In pairs or individually, class answers the questions on paper. The pieces of paper are sealed in an envelope that the class will not look at again until further on in the SoW

Notes and *questions for teachers*

Questions for part 1
- *Who holds knowledge?*
- *How is culture transmitted?*
- *What is the matter of those who work on the boundaries between the culture and the individual?*
- *What would the 'matter' be for your class of young people?*

'What is a myth?'written so that the class can see it
Establishing a base

Sharing knowledge, starting to find out about the class

Write the questions on the 'board' for ease of communication
What are the specifics of this need for ease in the classroom?
Protecting into understanding (what kind of culture is this? Bond)
A stab at recognising what we know, but no exposure
(This is what is known but not said)
Envelope – sign – *the secret ballot of teacher trade unionism?*
What other holding object could have been used?

Lesson 1: What is a myth? (continued)

Workshop participant's response: This was a metaphor for how we deal with unwanted truths. We are also here sealing away the unwanted truths of the group. We found it tantalising that these were going to appear later.

3. Teacher talk:

    'To reach the site of the ancient city of Troy one must take the car ferry from Gallipoli and cross the 'swift-flowing Hellespont' to the opposite bank at Canakkale (show on map or atlas).

    'Troy – for the ancients Troy was a real place – a citadel, according to Homer 'well-walled.' A 'broad city' with 'lofty gates', 'wide streets,' and 'fine towers'.

    The people of Troy *are** known as fine 'horse tamers' who take pride in their 'fine foals'.

    1250 years BC – the late Bronze Age

    At the heart of the citadel of Troy lies the temple of Apollo.

    The cult of Apollo is strong in this region. He is the chief deity. One who could be wild, cruel and rash in his youth. At one point he was almost expelled from Olympus by Zeus, but he learnt wisdom as he grew to maturity.

    In his temple at the heart of the citadel the novices *are* busy.

    They *are* preparing for the completion of their initiation.

4. Teacher-in-role:

    'Well my novices, my senior novices. Your labours are coming to fruition – and you have learnt your lessons well, some of you have even begun to take on pupils of your own.

    You have your basic tenets of the faith, you are almost ready to show the ways in which you follow, and what parts of the temple you are learning to be responsible for.

    But first you must prepare yourselves in these ways:

Notes and *questions for teachers*

The micro and the macro.

To set the scene further the teacher could read out first page of prologue from Michael Wood's *In Search of the Trojan War*

Map = sign

*Workshop participant's response: *are is a change of tense. We are being held in two worlds simultaneously: the real world of today and the fictional world of the myth. The change of tense edges us a little closer into the fiction we will create*

MH's reply: This juxtaposition of tense is, I think, important. It is one of the ways in which the teacher manipulates words in an almost poetic mode. The relationship between imagination and words is in play here in order to sign the shifting and blending between what we think the history is, what the myth says and our contemporary world.

'Is this true?'is a question I am frequently asked by children in Drama. The discussion that ensues will often hold the class's attention for quite some time as we try to unpick something of the relationship between history and myth, and what that reveals about human understanding, universal truths and historical 'facts'.

The poetic mode can provide us with a form for expressing and marking the boundaries, time-slips, and connections between then and now.

What reverberations are there in this story?

Introduction of role

Teacher in role (shadowy role). Shift in language, verbal and body. Alter pace and physical stance, use symbol. The class do not have to respond in role but they can if they want. The class is learning about its strengths, so nothing should be high stakes (the newness of the group).

The class will need to work out of role to read the Tenets* and to get to grips with the knowledge.

The tenets are with the resources at the end of the scheme.

Lesson 1: What is a Myth? (continued)

- You must read the Tenets one more time
- You must perform the ritual cleansing alone
- You must collect the keys that will open your part of the temple.
- You must ensure that you are ready to show the High Prophetai the ways in which you follow and what parts of the temple you are learning to be responsible for.

Now go and make ready.'

The class can each have a copy of the Tenets, fronted by these instructions in written form. Make sure that the class understand that priests are second only to the King.

Question to the class on the board:

What will we learn about the novices and their society as they go about their tasks?

5. Working alone or in small groups, the class create the matter of the temple, using papers, pens, candles, incense, objects. These can be indicated in advance with appropriate props in particular areas of the room.

Workshop participants' response: The choice of objects here was, we think, very important so should be given here. Handling these things took us into the 'other world' of the fiction. Reasons for choosing these particular parts of the temple would be useful as well.

MH's reply: When I first did this scheme of work with year 9 classes I allowed them to choose parts of the temple to work, as long as they related to that which Apollo was god of (see Tenets). They created the areas largely through drawing, with just one or two objects. Subsequently I have found that the work is deeper if I restrict these choices and offer more rigidity in this area of the SoW. I offer four areas I consider more tightly tied by threads of meaning to the significance of the story (see next column).

Notes and *questions for teachers*

The tenets are with the resources at the end of the scheme

Setting up the space: Iconic/symbolic levers

Parts of the Temple	Threads of meaning
The stables where the sacred horses are kept (NB: sacred – will be sacrificed?)	The wooden horse and the real horses/nature and control, death/ destruction and kinship with living things
Where the oracle is housed	Shadow and illumination, nature and artifice, manipulation of the material world, the covering and uncovering of meaning
Where the sacred water is kept	Water has a price at times of siege/ water cleanses /sacrificial animals must be cleansed/ oracle users must be cleansed
Where the tenets/laws are kept	The priests' relationship to government and power

There are some useful guiding principles for choosing objects:

Lesson 1: What is a Myth? (continued)

At some point during this work, the priests are given the keys to their areas. It is a matter of judgement whether the teacher uses it as a stimulus to help get groups going, or as a way of appointing particular participants to be leaders, or to show that each group 'owns' their area

Workshop participants' response: We thought the keys were highly significant both in our group and in the whole bathhouse scene, holding the contradictions of openness/secrecy, insiders/outsiders.

6. When all are ready:

a) Simultaneous depictions into action show the ritual cleansing – countdown by Teacher.

b) The parts of the temple are shown to the class/teacher as if they are the High Prophetai, or as if the High Prophetai is present.

   Teacher reflects the work of the class as they show.

c) At the end of the showing Tir as HP awards one participant the key to the communal bathhouse.

Notes and *questions for teachers*

■ They shouldn't be everyday

■ They should be universal enough to be invested with meaning within the drama and they should hold several possibilities; often easily found

Or

■ They should be highly specific to the story, searched out purposely

See also Tony Grady's article 'Romeo and Juliet' *Broadsheet* Vol 12, Issue 3

Stable

Found: straw, cloth to indicate area of stable, heads of horses (magnets), description of the relationship between miners and pit ponies

Searched out: ropes with special knots, fit to make knots, wooden image of horse that could be both toy and icon for stable keeper

Oracle

Found: red cloth, nightlights, essential oils, globe, rosemary plant, bay leaves, gold pottery bowl

Searched out: Computer and disc with possible information the oracle may give (this was never used)

Sacred Water

Found: sponge, urn, tap and sink in room, red cloth

Searched out: pottery goblets

Laws

Found: red tape, scrolls, chopsticks as stylos, chain of office

Searched out: slate that erases that which is written (I wanted a clay tablet, but made do with a child's 'magic slate'). The first rehearsed action is not shown to the class but *with* the class to the teacher.

This is a bridge to the showing of the next pieces.

It also pre-figures the bathhouse.

What kind of culture is this? Imagination is a form of materialism – Bond

Heightened, formal language? *

The class will develop a (shared) perspective of actions and behaviours

*MH: At this point in the workshop I spoke of the High Prophetai in the third person, trying to bring in echoes of the present for teachers. I said that the HP had noticed that

■ the guardians of the oracle are keeping their knowledge safe and one must enquire particularly to find it out

■ the law givers and makers are fervent and strong in the imparting of their knowledge

■ the guardians of the horses are in short supply

■ the water guardians need more sponges

Lesson 1: What is a Myth? (continued)

7. Whole class improvisation:

    After the completion the novices retire to the communal bathhouse.

    Questions to ask the class as the improvisation develops:

    What do they take with them? How do they step over the threshold? Who's first in the water? Who hangs back? What can be heard/smelt/felt?

    What do we learn about them and their society in this context?

Workshop participants' response

Some thoughts on the entry to the bathhouse:

The symbolism of the key was at work again. It gives a particular responsibility for the structuring of the drama for the next phase. In my case (the person to whom the key was given) it was also a 'gift' that enabled me to pause the whole class so I could 'read' how the class are, individually and collectively. My guess is that the participants were doing the same 'reading'. The pause makes it a real threshold into a new phase of the drama; actually the class is in charge, and in the fiction the novices are in charge, and therefore responsible. The bathhouse also allowed different types of acting behaviour, including that which was distinctive for different roles e.g. the stable keeper washing off the smell of horses.

MH: in the workshop the group were still being hesitant with each other here. I added in two questions:

■ *What is it is that is said?*

■ *What is it that is not being said?*

Teacher feeds back reflection on, and records, the world of the novices.

Notes and *questions for teachers*

Sign – restricted ownership – the awarding of access as a reward for success

Development of role
(Character investment questions)
A contrast to the holiness. A chance to be vulgar and explore sub-text
NB: The novices operate on the site of Nothingness, they are messengers and interpreters of it

Heightened, formal language reverberating through time

The answers to the questions were prepared in small groups and then shown/shared depending on the confidence of the group.

Lesson 2

1. Teacher tells the first part of the story:

    'According to Homer's Iliad, during the Trojan War, Hecuba and King Priam ruled the city of Troy. Now King Priam had many children, fifty sons some say.

    Amongst them all alone stood their daughter Cassandra, (or Alexandra as she was sometimes known), a beautiful young woman, blessed by Apollo with the gift of prophecy.

    But how was this gift imparted?

    A strange tale to our ears. In honour of the birthday of their twins, Cassandra and her brother Helenus, the king and queen celebrated in the temple of Apollo. The celebrations were exuberant and the intoxicated parents returned to their palace, leaving their beloved children sleeping in the temple. When their parents looked in on them the next morning, the children were entwined with serpents, which flicked their tongues into the children's ears.

    Thus was the gift of prophecy imparted.

    But it was not a pure gift.

    As we shall see.

    Cassandra grew, and like all noble children she took on the mantle of learning, becoming practised in the ways of Apollo. One night, exhausted by her practicing, she fell asleep in her god's temple. This time, however, Apollo came not with gifts, but for a reckoning. It is said that he was smitten with her.

    He tried to force himself upon her. She refused his advances, and he cursed her. He spat into her mouth and told her from that point on no one would believe her prophecies although they would, as ever, be true.'

    Pause for response from the class if needed.

2. Teacher talk:

    'As the novices go about their business, in their own parts of the temple, how do they attend to what is happening between Cassandra and Apollo?

    How can they defy the god – they are human?'

Notes and *questions for teachers*

Questions for part two

■   *What are the operant paradigms of the child?*

■   *How do these paradigms affect action/behaviour?*

■   *What kind of culture is this?*

culture must be a structure of meanings of the world which also understands itself as part of those meanings: it must be the means of interrogating and understanding itself (Bond)

Or else it is static/sterile a culture that is a means of survival is not a culture of change (becomes repressive and destructive).

Imagination expresses human value (Bond)

Workshop participants' response: being behind a closed door was a brilliant constraint. You couldn't intervene to idealistically change the story but you had to attend to what was going on.

MH's reply: I can't remember whether I specified that the novices had to be behind a closed door, but I think that this image of constraint might have been born out of the earlier use of keys

Lesson 2 (continued)

Depictions followed by small group improvisations to demonstrate answers to these questions.

3. Whole class individual improvisation – 'The novice priests prepare for their night's rest – what do they say in their prayers to Apollo that evening?' Spotlight.

Workshop participants' response: This enabled us to uncover stance.

4. Whole-class improvisation.

Teacher talk: 'The next day Cassandra comes to continue with her practice in the temple. Her usual tutor novice is indisposed. The novices meet to discuss who should teach her. How will her needs be met?'

The teacher could work in role as High Prophetai if the whole class improvisation needs guiding.

5. Group depictions with captions showing Cassandra's lesson. Represent Cassandra with paper feet showing where she is, moment to moment during the scene**.

6. Teacher talk:

'Cassandra grows in a time when truth is diminished. Her brother Paris is born and she tells her parents that the baby must be destroyed or it will bring about the downfall of Troy. Her warnings are not heeded, but her prophecy is fulfilled. The young Prince Paris is destined to fall in love with Helen, the beautiful wife of the Greek leader Menelaus. His view of what love is drives him to 'steal' her and bring her to Troy.

The next time we meet the novices they will be in the midst of war.'

Teaching Notes and *questions for teachers*

The mind is self-reflexive 'what is unseen around the corner' (Bond)

Here I intervened to stop two things happening:
- *The priests were beginning to scapegoat a particular priest who seemed to be being driven towards a personal collapse/crisis by the rigours of Apollo's priesthood*
- *The group was moving towards a vote to resolve the situation*

My reasoning was that
- *They shouldn't avoid this difficult child by dumping her on the priest least likely to cope*
- *I didn't want them to use democracy, and that I wanted later to make a learning point about democracy.*

Workshop participants' response: You're right! And, of course, constantly adult society is constantly trying to dump difficult children – exclusions, anti-social behaviour orders etc. But a species can't actually dump its young. They keep coming back: vandalising, mugging, breaking our rules just for the hell of it, getting pregnant, becoming soldiers who then turn on us...

** Tony Grady taught me this technique. It has proved useful time and again. It can protect the class – distance them and yet hold them in the moment.

Lesson 3

As the class enter – music: 'And the Band Played Waltzing Matilda'

1. Teacher talk

    'Sunrise on a besieged city.

    A province where thousands of years later the humans of the 21st century would stand to remember the battle of Gallipoli as the sun rises on Anzac day.

    Behind the hill on which Troy is built lies Mount Ida, and in front a plain sloping to the seashore. Through this plain run two beautiful rivers, and scattered here and there what you might take for steep knolls... they are mounds piled up over the ashes of warriors long ago dead.

    On these mounds stood the sentinels who saw the first approach of the Greek fleet as it drew near across the water.

    Read p.37 of *Tales of Troy and Greece* by Andrew Lang.

    'The God Apollo has visited pestilence on the Greeks. He supports his followers and the Trojans are not defeated. They were well prepared and their storerooms and pithoi are well filled. At least, the priests are well provided for.

    Ten years of siege'.

2. Small group prepared mime with thought tracking that answers the questions below. The characters are allowed one line of dialogue.

    ■ How does a city under siege honour its dead and take care of the living?

    ■ What are the novices doing?

    ■ What echoes are there from the mounds of the dead?

    Some suggestions for starters:

    Compiling a roll of honour for the dead

    What happens when someone comes to the temple door asking for help/supplies?

    What has happened to the horses?

    Who is Cassandra with?

    Show.

3. Reflection. The poem of the dead – each class member contributes a line.

Notes and *questions for teachers*

Question for lesson 3

How do people live in a besieged city and stay human?

*Workshop participants' response: This **song** is about world war one and particularly about those who are damaged by war but survive and bear witness about the world created after the war. In the drama we were dealing with the Trojan war; the conference was taking place during Bush and Blair's 'war on terrorism' and was attended by people from the aftermath of the war in the Balkans. In the drama, we are about to move to a sequence where questions about how a war is described, explained, and commemorated will be central. The quality of the song is both gentle (the tune) and brutal (the lyrics). The teacher never commented on it, but it had the effect of suddenly making all war present for us. This is a product, I think, of the aesthetics of the whole sequence – of how each past including the form of each past resonates with other parts and with the whole*

NB: Due to time constraints this is as far as the dialogue between the teacher participants and myself could go

Lesson 4

1. Read extract from *The Trojan Women* by Euripides describing the arrival of the horse and pulling it in.

    Discussion – questions.

    (Vocal warm up if needed)

2. Group sculpture – what actions do the novices take to express their joy that the war is now over?

    Depiction into action of the shout that went up in Troy – rehearse it. Then add in Cassandra, represented by paper feet.

3. Mark out a circle with rope.

    Pair work around the circle. A very short time to prepare, then each pair comes into the circle.

    Two at a time the novices present their gifts to the horse saying

    I bring greetings from...............

4. Whole class improvisation – 'the pulling in of the horse – the rope is fetched from the (now empty) stables of the sacred horses'.

    Guiding questions:

    'Where is the rope attached?

    Who knows how to attach it?

    Who stands where?

    How do they grasp the rope?

    How does it feel against the hand?

    What attention is paid to Cassandra?'

    Spotlight for thought tracking – 'as they pay no heed to Cassandra.'

5. Countdown to whole class depiction with spotlighting:

    'As the novices stand guard over the horse that night what answers do they think they've found?'

6. Teacher reads out extract from *The Trojan Women* describing what happens when the Greeks emerge from the horse.

7. Reflective task demonstrated with the whole class and then worked on in small groups – teacher demonstrates how to cut a spiral from a piece of sugar paper. Teacher talk 'if we could unpick the strands of the rope what words and ideas would we find hidden there?' Write them on the spirals.

    Share. Display.

Notes and *questions for teachers*

Question for lesson 4

How *is Cassandra's warning ignored?*

Before the lesson, write out Cassandra's words of warning about the horse, large enough for the class to see

Have ready a rope, sugar paper, scissors and pens

Put questions on the board

Possible use of extracts from *Report from Ground Zero*

This culture does not question itself – it is static – (is this why it dies?)

Nothingness – it is human construct expressed in matter

Reflective words framed by the matter used to bring about action.

Lesson 4 (continued)	**Notes and *questions for teachers***
8. Teacher narrates: 'As the sun sets the following day I wonder what is there to see and hear upon the streets of the city? I wonder what has become of the rope that pulled the Trojan horse in the city?' NB: Democracy is on its way.	These questions are for the final context. They are left hanging
2. Teacher sets scene for depiction-action-depiction: 'The priests are dead. The novices are in charge of the temple. What will they do now? What questions are there to ask of the oracle?' Show.	Reflective action moving towards future action – the possible
3. Return to the envelope. Read out what was written. Reflection: What do we know and what do we need to know?	

Resources

Three kinds of resources were used:

- stories, histories
- objects
- information

The first two are clearly identified in the scheme above. The third, i.e. the Tenets, was gleaned and adapted from the web (where I discovered that worship of Apollo still goes on). They are used in part one of the scheme of work. How much the teacher chooses to use will depend on the class. It may be preferable to ask the class to create their own tenets.

NB: I also collected several images and media extracts cataloguing the unfolding events of war at that time. I had them ready on disc, with a computer set up for use as a possible manifestation of the oracle. In the event, it was not used.

Song
Bogle, Eric *The Band Played Waltzing Matilda*, sung by June Tabor, Anthology Music Club

The Tenets

You must know that Apollo is a god of many things.

- prophesy
- visions
- divination,
- healing and medicine,
- archery
- law and order
- the arts, sciences, music, and writing.

Apollo has many names: Pythios, Delphinian, Loxias, Phoebus (Greek Phoibos), Far-Darter, Distant Deadly Archer, Lukeios (Wolfish), Iatros (Physician), and Daphnephoros (Bay-Bearer).

His animals are the crow, the raven, the dolphin, the lion, the hawk and the swan.

The Creed

- Know thyself
- Nothing too much
- Avoid hubris

The Ways in Which We Follow:

- Keepers of the Sacred Waters
- Guardians and interpreters of the Oracle
- Keepers of the sacred horses
- Guardians and makers of the laws

CASSANDRA (THE PRIESTS) ■

Keepers of the Sacred Waters

Far beneath our sacred temple we house the source of the Ayazma that waters Mount Ida, the throne of the Trojan Gods. The Ayazma is itself the source of the divine Scamander River, descended from Zeus.

Guardians and Interpreters of the Oracle

We follow the tradition of the great Pythia at Apollo's oracle at Delphi, where in the very navel of the universe, in the hallowed chamber below the great temple where the sacred vapours flow from earth, the Pythia answers the questions of the future.

She who would be Apollo's mouthpiece must be pure.

The mouth of the oracle must be knowledgeable in many areas: history, religion, geography, politics, mathematics, philosophy, etc. She utters advice on where and how to build cities, which laws to incorporate, and which prayers to offer. Her predictions must be strategically attained and phrased, or supplicants may misinterpret the advice (remember Croesus*).

Keepers of the Sacred Horses

On the morning of a day when prophecy is scheduled, a horse must be sacrificed to the river and its entrails examined. If results are favourable the Oracle must operate that day.

Guardians and Makers of the Laws

We must uphold the Tenets.

On the morning of a day when prophecy is scheduled there must be:

purification in the Ayazma waters, and dress in full ceremonial robes.

Each pilgrim must pose a question to one of the Prophetai, who then relay it to the mouth of the oracle.

*   King Croesus asked whether he should launch an attack against the mighty Persians. Pythia told him that if he did he would 'destroy a great empire.' When Croesus' attack leads to his total annihilation by the Persians, he returned angry and full of protest to the oracle. The Pythia told him that her oracle had come true – he was simply too blind to read it correctly. He was forced to accept the word of Apollo.

The Facility

A scheme of work arising from the myth of Lycaon

Introduction

This scheme began to take shape during work with a year 11 GCSE Drama class. We were working from a stimulus – an extract from a play based on George Orwell's *Animal Farm* sent by the exam board (OCR).

We began by exploring the nature of the relationship between humans and animals. The class loved watching Desmond Morris' *The Human Animal,* and were very interested in the differences and similarities between humans and animals. They surprised me with their knowledge of and affection for animals. As the examination course requires the students to devise and present a performance arising from this stimulus, I designed tasks to help them make decisions about form. I was surprised at how much they enjoyed acting animals and the animal in the human.

I took some of the ideas that had emerged in the year 11 class and developed them into work with year 9 classes. Here the wolves came to the fore. I was able to include an extract from a novel I had long wanted to use, describing the smell of a soul. This light-hearted novel features werewolves who, when in wolf form, kill humans – but only global capitalists.

At the same time this scheme of work was coming into being we were being bombarded with images, words and knowledge of the war in Iraq and America's 'War on Terrorism'.

Thus this SoW was prepared with, so partly written by, the pupils I teach, and brought, almost finished, to the 2004 NATD conference. At the conference, the teachers' work enabled me to bring it to conclusion.

For this SoW the physicalisation/ representations of the material world are emboldened, and the theatrical moments that can underpin the teaching are underlined.

As ever, the writings of Bruner, Heathcote and Bond influenced me:

'*imagination is a form of materialism*'
Edward Bond Modern *Drama and the Invisible Object*

'*the materials of education are chosen for their amenableness to imaginative transformation*'
Jerome Bruner

'*sitting there and imagining it doesn't have enough praxis in it*'
Contexts for Active Learning by Dorothy Heathcote

Other key influences on this SoW are the works of Richard Dawkins, Robin Dunbar, Charlotte Uhlenbroek and Barry Holstun Lopez.

LYCAON

(This is one version – there's a simpler version in Barry Holstun Lopez's book)

There once a king of the ancient land of Arcadia – his name was Lycaon and he was the father of fifty sons. Now, one day Zeus, the king of the gods, heard a rumour that Lycaon and his sons were some of the most arrogant and disrespectful people on this planet.

Zeus decided to go and see for himself. He disguised himself as a humble traveller, and arrived at Lycaon's palace at dusk. It was time for the evening meal and Lycaon had gathered his huge family at the table. When he saw that there was an uninvited stranger at his table, and a humble one at that, King Lycaon was hostile. 'Who are you, and what do you want here?'

The humble traveller responded. ' I am an immortal god, and I seek hospitality in the name of far-seeing Zeus, who is the protector of strangers and beggars.'

At this, Lycaon looked at the traveller and grinned. 'We will see,' he said. 'You look more like a mortal to me. However, I invite you to share part of our meal with us. I must go and make arrangements for the meal – we must make a special sacrifice as we have a guest.'

While he was out of the room Lycaon arranged for a change to the menu. The usual meat was to be substituted by, if you can believe it, human flesh. One of his own grandsons, in fact. He knew that if their strange guest was a god, he would not touch it.

Lycaon placed the meat in front of his guest.

The stranger looked at his plate with complete contempt – and he began to change.

Meanwhile, the rest of the royal family had forgotten his presence as they ravenously attacked the food upon their plates, and so they did not witness the transformation that was occurring only a few feet away.

By the time they felt the tremendous heat and the blinding white light, it was too late to escape. Zeus, no longer in disguise, overturned the feast and rocked the palace with a wild thunderstorm. Lightning bolts struck the roof and walls, overwhelming the palace with raging flames and killing every occupant except Lycaon.

Lycaon fled from his palace and hid in the fields. The darkness and the cool breeze felt good upon his skin. He opened his mouth to call out, but his tongue would not obey his mind. All he could do was howl.

Terror struck, Lycaon examined himself. He was suddenly aware that instead of running as he usually did; he was using his arms as well as his legs. He found that he no longer could stand upright. His skin and robes had become covered with long hairs of silver and grey. As he licked his dry lips, he could see a longer, more pointed tongue. He had become a wolf!

Zeus commanded that if Lycaon wanted to return to human form he had to refrain from consuming human flesh for three years.

Lesson 1: What kind of creature is a human being?

Notes

1. Teacher talk 'we will be working from at least two viewpoints:
   - ■ as drama students- students of the human condition who may be able to approach a curriculum for living through their drama
   - ■ in role, creating a drama together

We will use ancient and new wisdom, imagination and reason to approach three questions – we may alter these questions as we go:
What kind of creature is a human being?
What is the human condition?
When did we become human?

We are going to begin as students of the human condition by watching extracts from a video of Desmond Morris' television series *The Human Animal.*

2. Teacher focuses class as they watch extracts from the video on
   - ■ that which is different
   - ■ that which is the same

between animals and humans. Teacher records this on sugar paper and pins the 'findings' up on the wall. They represent a first stab at reflection on what it is to be human. They should be seen not as conclusive but as exploratory.

3. Teacher tells the class that the ancient Greeks had their own way to explain the difference between animals and humans:

'Greek myths say that at the beginning of the world, long before man existed, the earth was ruled over by gods known as Titans. Their king, Cronus was wild and cruel but his son Zeus brought his rule to an end. The whys and wherefores, the hows and the whos of that violent tale belong to another story. Our story now tells of two Titans who could see which way the wind was blowing. They were brothers, Prometheus and Epimetheus, and they supported the rebellious Zeus, helping to make him the new king of the gods.

Now the earth lacked only two things: humans and animals.

Prometheus it was who made the first men, out of clay. His brother Epimetheus created the animals. As Epimetheus worked he gave each animal a gift from the gods.

Before the lesson spread out on a table or have on the walls **pictures and books/magazines with pictures of animals**

I often have music playing as the class enters. Students who arrive promptly can look at the pictures while the rest of the class arrive

I found copies of the **video** of this TV series (from the mid 1990s) through the world wide web. Its particular strengths are that Desmond Morris speaks of the human species as members of the animal world, and also of our unique qualities. NB: There is one particularly noteworthy section of the video that shows how children all over the world follow the same developmental pattern when they draw

If you cannot get this video, you could use other videos of nature programmes. Make sure that you draw out the 'animal' qualities of humans as you discuss the differences with your class.

Have written on board in advance:

'I would like to remind you that Timberlake Wertenbaker has said that a myth is '*an unwanted truth* reverberating down through time.'

This quotation refers to two schemes of work *The Cooks in the Kitchen* in year 8, and *Cassandra (The Priests)* in year 9.

This story refers to a year 7 scheme of work, *Prometheus*.

Lesson 1: What Kind of Creature is a Human Being?

Notes

After Epimetheus had completed his work, Prometheus finished making the people. However when he went to see what gift to give them, Epimetheus shamefacedly informed him that he had foolishly used up all the gifts.

Distressed, Prometheus decided he had to give the people fire, even though only the gods were meant to have it. As the sun god rode out into the world the next morning, Prometheus took some of the fire and brought it back the people. Of all the gifts the ancient ones could have presented to the people this was the one that made the difference. The fire that lit the way into a whole new future. The fire that gave us the questions.

Thus the ancient Greeks expressed the difference.'

One of my year 11 students said

'You know what the difference is between animals and us is Miss? – it's *why*'

Edward Bond has written:

'An animal is a human without a text'(5)

Teacher talk:

'We're going to move forward now, into that future thousands of years later. A future, in the 21st century where, it might seem, the people stand on the edge of their knowledge. We're going to get to know a particular group of people living and working in the 21st century. A particular group of people who will have some important decisions to make'.

Possible extension work:

'And what of us? What is it that makes us human? Maybe it's more a question of when than what?' Research task for students.

Give out – *When did we become human?* (see resources).

Lesson 2: What Kind of a Human Being is a Keeper?

1. Give out copies of **Job Advertisement** – (see resources)

    Teacher talk: 'imagine that you are someone who has seen this advertisement in the paper, and it is just what you have been looking for – the very job! You cut the advert out and apply for the post – as you fill out the application form you think about your qualifications and experience, and the whole reason you started working with animals'.

    Teacher begins to spotlight one or two pupils asking them about their (beginning) character's background.

    Additional activity – the class could complete the job application forms (see resources).

2. The interview the teacher organises the class into an improvisation wheel. The class forms into an inner and outer circle, facing each other in pairs. As the interview progresses they rotate, with the inner circle staying still and the outer circle moving on one place. Teacher tells the class that they will be taking it in turn to play two characters, alternating between interviewer and interviewee.

    Write three questions on paper or on the board (see resources)

    ■ When did you first realise that you had a skill and/or empathy with animals?

    ■ Why is working with animals important?

    ■ What things must you keep in mind to handle animals correctly?

    The inner circle begin as interviewers and the outer as interviewees. When they have had time to have a stab at the interview, the outer circle stand up and move round one. The interview is repeated, this time with teacher spotlighting – 'would you employ this person? Why?'

    The exercise is repeated, with the interviewers and the interviewees changing roles.

    Teacher feeds in 'rigour' of the demands of the Facility to keep the characters believable as they come into being.

    > Teacher given questions.

    > Put up **collages** for the four projects

3. Teacher talk 'The candidates are all successful. On the appointed day the personnel officer, Ms Andrews meets them at the Facility.'

    *Teacher-in-role as Ms Andrews, she has in her hand a **dog whistle** – Ms Andrews always carries this but doesn't speak of it (unless questioned by the class).*

    > Personnel Manager: the 'keeper' of the employees?

    'Here at the facility we have four main projects, covering 28 acres above ground and extending two layers below ground level. The four main projects are:

    2/98 – which works mostly with primates

    Lycaon – which works mostly with wolves

    The Ark which works with rare animals – have a precious tiger at the moment

    Keystone – which works mostly with predators.

Lesson 2: What Kind of a Human Being is a Keeper? (continued)

Our animals are very well cared for, and each of the four main projects is housed in a large environment entirely designed to provide as natural a habitat as possible. The observation posts are blended in to the environment, as is the CCTV.'

Teacher-in-role describes the personnel mess, shows them where their lockers are, mentioning that she thinks these have all been cleaned out. She indicates other amenities and explains that they will all begin in the Lycaon Project but will, over time, be rotated – 'mustn't get too attached to the animals – too much trouble with that in the past'. (Make sure the class hears this but if they question it explain that it's all in the past and not relevant to them and move on quickly).

'Any questions?'

If this is at the end of a lesson, teacher could ask the class to think about **what the keepers might bring** to put in their lockers when they start work next day.

4. Teacher says:

'As the new keepers begin to put their **things** in their lockers they catch the faintest **whiff of an unsettling smell**, masked by disinfectant and air fresheners'. Freeze

5. Devise and show pair scenes – short overheard conversations as the new keepers put their **things** (mimed) in their lockers:

– What do we learn about the keepers?

– What are their senses telling them

– What do they think about each other?

As these are shown, reflect on these questions and what the **objects** in the lockers tell us about the characters.

Notes

I created 4 **collages** – and 4 clearly labelled **folders** – one for each project, showing the kinds of animals in each project – they represent the physicality of the projects

NB: form – the lockers are mimed – if the students want to use real objects, or representations of real objects, they can't put them in the (mimed) lockers – they have to solve this problem or mime everything

Lesson 3: What Kind of a Creature is a Wolf?

Notes
Put up **wolf pictures** – I laminated 12 A3 photos of wolves from an old calendar

Each group has some scientific info about wolves. I find the book *Of Wolves and Men* by Barry Holstun Lopez very useful for factual information on wolves, or the school library may have good information

1. Teacher talk –

   'And so the keepers settle to their work – their daily routines begin to be established – they all begin in the Lycaon project. They must both care for and observe the wolves.'

   Small groups prepare 3 depictions of daily life. They can represent the positioning of the wolves with **wolf paw prints**.

   Teacher demonstrates different ways the wolf paw prints can be used – four paw prints = one wolf. For example they can be laid out flat on the floor, as though the wolf is standing, or two can be put on a chair, and two on the floor to show that the wolf is rearing up.

2. Teacher asks the groups to show, simultaneously, their three depictions. This is repeated and refined as they re asked to move from one depiction to the next to the count of 8 beats. This process continues to be repeated and refined. Music or syncopated words can be added depending on the class.
   Show.

   Teacher talk: 'And so time passes in the daily rhythm of the work and the care. And below the rhythm that is familiar, the rhythm that can dull the senses, there is still the **faintest whiff of an unsettling smell**, masked by disinfectant and air fresheners.

   And so the keepers, in 2004, come to know the wolves'.

3. And what of the ancient Greeks and wolves? What did they have to say about them?

   Teacher recounts the myth of Lycaon (above).

Lesson 4: What is the Human Condition?

1. *As the class enter, an extract from Talking with Animals is playing (see sources). It shows the naturalist Charlotte Uhlenbroek talking with and about wolves. The sound is muted and the class hears music:* track 9 from the CD *The Long Journey Home* by Peter Gabriel. Should it prove difficult to find these resources, this theatrical moment could be managed with e.g. a coat with a paw print on it.

   Teacher says: 'what you can know, but the keepers do not, is that there was a keeper once who worked at the facility, who knew a great deal about the wolves. She doesn't work there now.

2. And in the Facility? Well, as I have said – time passes in the daily rhythm of the work and the care. And below the rhythm that is familiar, the rhythm that can dull the senses, there is still the faintest whiff of an unsettling smell, masked by disinfectant and air fresheners.'

   The keepers begin to find things out.

   The teacher asks the class to work in 3 groups, listing the objects/tools they use in their daily work. As they make this list, teacher goes around the groups revealing a hidden 'object' to each group, and asking them to create a scene that shows what the keepers do when they discover these 'objects'.

   – **a muzzle**, that has a strangely human smell – found when taking out their tools one morning

   – **a burnt notebook** with some surviving burnt pages (see resources) – found when taking out their tools one morning

   – an i**mage** of a woman who looks as though she is talking to a wolf, glimpsed in the moonlight by a keeper as he tidies away tools at the end of a late shift.

3. Show and reflect – what do we notice now about these keepers?

4. Group task on sugar paper – as the keepers fill in their **daily log** at the end of their shift, will it be a true record or will there be omissions? Share.

5. Teacher talk and teacher demonstration, narrating her own actions:

   'There is something else to notice too- a corner, protruding from a shadow. *A keeper reaches out to prod it into view – a tape, belonging to the CCTV – on it a label half destroyed – all that can be seen are the words* **Interview With a W...**'

   'But that will have to wait for the next lesson.'

Notes

Before the lesson hide the three objects in the room, each in an area where you will ask a group to work. Also, have a video with *Interview with a W...* written on the cover and hide this in the room too.

This image is created by the silhouette of a wolf cut out in black sugar paper and attached to the wall – the teacher depicts the woman speaking to it.

Sometimes the class call out what the W might stand for: 'woman', 'wolf'. This heightens their anticipation.

Part 5: What Kind of Creature is a Werewolf?

Notes

1. Teacher asks class to recap the end of previous lesson.

   Re- place 'Interview with a W......'

   Whole-class depiction – what will the keepers do with this tape? Where and how might they watch it?

   Teacher says 'Show me whether your character will watch this videotape or turn their back on it'. Class brings depiction to life for 10 seconds.

   Teacher summarises whether or not all of the keepers, or just one of them, will watch the video, and the classroom is set up accordingly e.g. one pupil sitting in the middle of the circle watching.

2. Teacher tells the class – 'The title of this tape is *Interview with a Werewolf*. On the tape the former keeper is asking a wolf questions, and, if you can believe it, the wolf is answering them. What questions do you think the former keeper is asking the wolf?'

   In pairs the class plan the questions the former keeper asked the werewolf and reports them back to the teacher, who can scribe them if necessary.

   Teacher talk – 'You will now be playing two people again. As a group you will ask the questions the former keeper asked the werewolf. You are also the keeper(s), watching the videotape *Interview With a Werewolf.*'

3. *Tir speaks the voice of werewolf as the class ask questions.* During the questioning the Tir reveals that:

   She is female and a soldier in the army. She is not the only one – there is a whole battalion in The Facility, hidden away. Her memory is hazy on some things because of the drug Ketamine that is used to subdue the wolves. She was in a war, somewhere hot. Her battalion was 'volunteered' by the army for a special project. They were given injections and, over time, transformed into wolves. They were sent out on night-time missions and were very good at it – swift and deadly – sometimes as wolf sometimes as human. As time passed it became increasingly difficult to return to human form and eventually they got stuck in wolf form. They are an embarrassment to the army now and brought back to England and put in the Facility. She wants to regain her human form and return to her family. She has a child. She is angry and despairing – desperate to be human again.

   If asked about Ms. Andrews, say that she stinks – but what she carries in her hand makes the wolves fearful of her.

   If asked if the werewolf would harm the keepers, say not if they have the right smell.

   When the teacher feels enough questions have been asked, she comes out of role speedily and says with urgency:

   'Footsteps are heard, the tape is switched off and secreted away – it is the end of the shift – the keepers go home.'

4. Whole class depiction to action – how do the keepers leave the Facility?

I set up a wolf head that has eyes that light up, and sit next to it. You could use a large picture of a wolf, spotlight (with a torch?) or just play it

Tir placing wolf's paw prints below your feet.

Lesson 6: When Did We Become Human?

1. Teacher talk:

    'It is the start of the next shift. On the way into work the keepers see this **picture** in their newspapers.

    Copies of the picture are laid on the floor in front of the class.

    Notes

    In advance, write up the piece about the flute on the board and cover it up

    Having the picture small requires the pupils to peer at it

    The class goes straight into class depiction:

    'as the keepers are at their lockers, what is there to notice about them (the keepers)?

    If the wolf was there to describe the smell of their souls, what would it be?'

    Pupils come out of the depiction one at a time and say what they notice and what the wolf would smell.

2. Teacher uncovers these words:

    It is said that that which drives the life's blood of human culture is storytelling and music.

    The earliest humans had music.

    *On an ancient site in Slovenia a **flute** made from bone was found. From the bone of a bear. This flute is 53,000 years old.*

3. Teacher places a question to be answered with small group improvisations: 'how can the keepers help the werewolves be human again?'

4. Concluding task: two depictions one year on
    –   Where are the werewolves now?
    –   Where are the humans now?

5. Teacher asks reflective questions:

    'What kind of creature is a human being?

    Are there any questions you want to ask now?'

Some ending scenes suggested by pupils:

■ Will the next generation be wolf cubs or human babies?

■ Put aside fear and be alongside the werewolves to model human behaviour to them.

■ Keep developing the science to find a chemical remedy.

■ No quick fix – be their friend

■ Help them come to terms with being werewolves as there is no going back and keep them caged.

■ Help them come to terms with being werewolves and let them out to be free.

■ The song of the human

Resources

Video – Desmond Morris *The Human Animal*
Facility advert
Job application form
List of four projects
Epimetheus myth
Lycaon myth
Questions for job interview
Pictures for each project
Wolf pictures
3 pieces of information on wolves
Burnt notebook clues/ Words from the ashes
Shadow/silhouette of woman talking to a wolf

Interview with a werewolf video tape cover (mock up)
Coat/ tape of former keeper
CD *The Long Journey Home* – Peter Gabriel (13)
'When did we become human' sheet draft
Soldier picture

Sources:

See introduction

BBC Wildlife magazine for excellent wildlife pictures.

When did we become human? Working document – draft

1. Please see if you can replace some of the question marks with dates.
2. Can you find information to put into the empty rows?

Roughly:

? million years ago, when dinosaurs held sway	Primate family appears. Our earliest ancestors skittered through the trees and bushes, much as squirrels do today
	Ancestors of monkeys and apes appeared
5-7 million years ago	Human – ape ancestors.
4 million years ago	Bipedal, human-like species
2 million years ago	Homo erectus appears – dramatic improvement in quality and range of tools – very simple hand axes.
	Third order intentionality appears?
	Controlled use of fire?
	Two species of chimp separate
	Brain doubles in size
500,000 years ago	Homo Sapiens – larger brain, lighter body build
	Fourth order intentionality appears?
150,000 – 200,000 years ago	Anatomically modern humans .
	Fifth order intentionality?
	Small group of about 5000 females (and about the same number of males) living in Africa from whom all five billion of us modern humans have descended
50,000 years ago (about 100, 000 years after the human brain reaches its modern size)	Upper Palaeolithic Revolution – sudden change – knifelike blades, borers, arrowheads,
28,000 years ago	Neanderthals die out
20,000 years ago	Awls, needles, Venus figurines
18,000 years ago	Cave paintings
?	
?	

THE ANIMAL FACILITY
TAF is an international research centre working to develop the
health and understanding of animals worldwide

Technician, Animal Keeper – Animal Facility

Salary/Wage:	6.50-15.00 Eu/hour
Status:	Full Time, Part Time, Employee
Shift:	First Shift (Day), Second Shift (Afternoon), Third Shift (Night), Rotating
Company:	The Animal Facility
For further details and an application form contact:	Ms Andrews The Human Resources Department
Email:	amcsk@earthlink.com
Address:	Brightways Laboratory 83 Stoke Blvd, Stoke Stamford NIL 607
Phone:	847-773-2616
Fax:	847-673-3121

Job Description

Seeking friendly, enthusiastic individuals who enjoy interacting with people and animals. Openings available in assisting the research, and animal care. Work in a modern spacious animal Facility with other dedicated staff members who promote a friendly team environment.

The pension scheme is similar to the Civil Service scheme with a nominal contribution from employees. Annual leave is 25 days on appointment plus 10.5 days public and privilege holidays. The Facility has subsidised child care/nursery schemes, staff restaurants and free parking.

Please quote reference number **05P/2002**

Name:

Post Applied for:

Experience

Education

Interests

Supporting Statement

Contact Details

Interview Questions

When did you first realise that you had a skill or empathy with animals?

Why is working with animals important?

What things must you keep in mind when handling animals correctly?

Words in the burnt notebook – or could be just fragments of burnt paper:

We must return to Lycaon,
for there we will

Whenever the new moon
the restlessness
inescapable patterns
genetic course

Lycanthropic Metamorphic Disorder
control with **Ketamine**

- this drug produces a feeling of being separated from your body, numbness and then deep sedation, sluggish
- may cause memory loss
- highly addictive
- can lead to a K hole – hallucinatory state,
- may cause you to stop breathing – on high doses you have to have an endotracheal tube inserted to help you breathe

Interview with a werewolf

'*Every soul has a unique smell and this one smelled of enthusiastic compromises with dictators, devious ambition, greed, lost children.*

This smell was not detectable by normal humans, but if they could have smelled it, they would have been overcome by the stench of wormy meat that had been kept in a dirty sock in the hot sun for a week or so, then set afloat in petroleum.

It took one snap to break his neck'. (Hayter 2002)

Section Three

Schemes for years 10 and 11

What's Theatre For?

A scheme of work exploring censorship and two script extracts

Introduction

Preparing work for students taking GCSE examinations can pose several challenges to the drama teacher. One concerns the GCSE units that require students to study script extracts, rather than whole plays. Taking an extract out of a whole play goes against the artistic grain, so the struggle for the teacher is to try to create a scheme that will both resonate something of the content of the plays and introduce the students to the artistic existence of key playwrights in a creative way.

This scheme of work juxtaposes extracts from *Saved* and *Mountain Language* with the world of the drama students in school, and actors outside school. It raises the question of what theatre is for. I have used this work chiefly with year 10 GCSE groups. It works both on text and off.

The whole class role-play in lesson 3 is based on an actual event – something that happened to me as a young teacher. I was preparing a lesson based on *Saved* and a school secretary saw the script (but not the lesson plan). She said nothing, but went to the headteacher and complained that such a play was being studied in school. The head teacher called me into her office and asked why I was working with such material. I showed her my lesson plan, and she was satisfied.

In June 1996 a group of London-based Kurdish actors began rehearsals for a revival of *Mountain Language*. They hired a community centre in London, near where I live, in which to rehearse. For their production they obtained military uniform and plastic guns from the National Theatre. A local resident contacted the police when he saw what he thought was a group of armed men entering the Kurdish community centre. The police despatched a helicopter, stationed marksmen with automatic rifles on an adjoining roof, and besieged the building. The actors were handcuffed and interrogated, and forbidden to communicate with one another in their native Kurdish. Eventually the police understood what was actually going on and allowed the production to go ahead.

Text 1: *Saved* by Edward Bond

Lesson 1: The Teenage Mother

Notes

1. Teacher explains that the class will be pursuing a practical study of text, and that it will begin with off text work on an extract of Edward Bond's *Saved.*

2. Teacher asks the class, working individually, to spread out around the room, and begin to build a depiction a parent of a fifteen year old girl, 'sitting in the daughter's room – she is not at home at the moment – in your hand is a small plastic tube – you have found it in your daughter's room – it is a used pregnancy test kit – it reads positive. Create an action – depiction – action to show what your hand does with the kit'.

   Teacher gives the students time to rehearse this and then asks the class to show their individual action – depiction – actions simultaneously, half the class at a time, with the other half watching.

3. Teacher focuses the class on discussion of what the hands were doing and how, and what implications there are for the young mother-to-be and her baby?

4. Teacher says: 'Time moves on, as it must, and the young mother is leaving the maternity ward.'

   Teacher organises the building of a depiction in the circle – 'How is she carrying the baby? What does this tell us about her? What does she need? What does the baby need? If the young mother's needs could speak what would they say? If the baby's needs could speak, what would they say? What is waiting for them as they step out into the world?'

5. Teacher asks the class to create short scenes, using thought-tracking for the baby and the mother, and the world outside, showing them as they step out of the hospital.

6. As the groups show their work, teacher focuses the discussion on what is being demonstrated about the responsibilities humans have for the care/'thriving' of one another?

Edging into a world of violence and inhumanness, this first exercise deliberately begins with something relatively safe and easy – teenage pregnancy is the stuff of television soap operas and so, in my experience of teaching diverse classes of 14/15 year olds, it feels like familiar territory – something that the class thinks is acceptable for public discussion. The class are cast in the role of parents in order to lend some distance from themselves as teenagers - teenage pregnancy is not just a fiction; it is something to be treated with care in the secondary school.

Lesson 2: The Script Extract

Notes

1. Ask the pupils if there are any questions arising from the previous lesson.

   Try to draw out the situation of the baby and its parents.

2. Introduce the work of Edward Bond.

   The pupils should be encouraged to make a few brief notes (see resources).

3. Teacher reads out an introduction to the script, and points out the language and the dialect, explaining how it's pronounced – the class reads scene 6.

4. Teacher focuses discussion on the 'questions/concerns we would raise if we were going to perform this in a theatre today'.

5. Teacher organises the class into groups, asking them to portray moments of media reaction to Bond's play when it was first staged. The groups can:

   ■ Pick 3 or 4 key moments from the scene to show as photos that might have appeared in the press in 1965, with captions or headlines.

   ■ Create an extract that was shown on TV which fuelled the debate – bring one of the photos to life as a TV extract and include the TV commentators' comments.

6. As the groups show back their 'moments', Teacher focuses the discussion on why EB wrote the play.

It's important that EB is recognised as an established, committed playwright, whose work is concerned with humanness

Not all students find it easy to read the dialect in which Bond wrote this play

It's important that you think through your own reactions to this scene

Lesson 3: Intervention

Notes

1. Teacher explains that the class are going to be working in role as a class of year 12s who are studying to put on a production of *Saved* as part of their 'A' level examination.

   Teacher tells them that she is going to be in role as someone from outside the school, and asks for a volunteer to work in role as the head teacher, and another as the class drama teacher.

2. Teacher prepares the class for their roles by asking them to decide what the differing attitudes the year 12s are to their studies.

   Teacher sets up the action for a whole class role-play, and explains that the year 12 class are working in groups and the class teacher is going round helping them prepare their scenes.

   As the class begins this exercise, Teacher briefs the pupil taking on the role of the head teacher about teacher's role – that of a parent who has discovered her son/daughters' script at home and is disturbed that they should be working on such a violent and upsetting play – Tir is about to go into the class to protest and the headteacher is hot on Tir's heels trying to calm her down.

You could give the pupil taking on the role of class drama teacher a simple, concrete task such as asking the groups what props or lights they might want.

Lesson 3: Intervention (continued)

As this role-play is enacted, Tir guides the pupils into dealing effectively with the situation, and enables it to come to a satisfactory conclusion (in terms of dramatic tension).

3. Having concluded the role-play, teacher focuses the class on the different characters' points of view.

4. Teacher asks the class to work in pairs to create a scene showing: 'That evening as the year 12s go home and learn lines or make props, what are they thinking about the play? What discussions might they have about the play with the folks at home?'
Show.

Homework / written task:

The year 12 class decide that they want to put on a performance of *Saved* or, rather, an extract from it for a particular audience – who? How will they perform it?

Or

The year 12 class must still put on a performance for their examination. What will this be about? How will they perform it?

Notes

Don't be nervous of stopping and re-working aspects of the role-play if needs be. There is no one correct ending to this scene – it will depend on the needs of the class – usually most of the students fight hard to maintain their right to perform this play

Depending on the ending of the role-play, this task might be:

'That evening the year 12s go home-as they tear up their scripts or throw away the props what are they thinking about the play? What discussions might they have with the folks at home about the play?

Text 2: *Mountain Language* by Harold Pinter

Lesson 4: The Script

1. Teacher introduces playwright, Harold Pinter (see resources) and class reads scenes one and two of *Mountain Language*. Discuss the impact of the banning of the language on the women a) waiting and b) visiting.
Teacher explains that the class is going to be working 'off the text'.

2. In circle, Teacher asks the class to imagine a powerful city, 10 years from now and focuses the discussion on what its main characteristics could be – 'What words do they particularly use in this city?'

3. Teacher asks class to spread out around the room and create individual depictions of life in the city e.g.
'On the way to work – what do you have on you?'. Teacher notes the words used.
Teacher develops this into whole class spontaneous improvisation, simultaneously beginning with mime and developing through hot-seating for thoughts, attitudes and preoccupations.

4. Teacher asks class to develop group scenes showing typical scenes of the city at work – 'What words do they use that tell us something important about their way of life?'
As the groups show their work, Teacher notes the words used.
Homework/written task: Sketch and label the city.

Lesson 5: The Mountain People

1. Teacher says – 'We are now going to shift location to a village in the mountains of the same country at the same time.

   Teacher asks class to create group depictions: 'The villagers are putting away their tools at the end of the day'. Teacher asks groups to develop this work by adding a narrator who describes what the villagers are doing, and showing how the words of the mountain people contrast with those of the city.

   Show.

2. Teacher countdown to a whole class freeze: 'The people of the village are called to their village square. A government representative, in uniform, has an announcement to make.' Tir reads out the text extract (see resources) and enables a whole class role-play.

   Teacher explains that she will read the speech again and ask for one word from each pupil – 'what is the single most important word that they cannot now speak?' Tir reads speech again.

3. Teacher asks class to work in small groups preparing a series of news bulletins showing 2 or 3 events in the days leading up to this pronouncement.

   As the groups present the bulletins, Teacher might want to use 'rewind' to investigate moments more closely. Also, Teacher notes what opportunities or questions are being raised by the pupils' work that will guide the next section of the work

   e.g.

   ■ Have mountain people and city people always lived side by side?

   ■ Are there opportunities for people who speak both languages?

   ■ What is the status of the bilingual person? To which side do they owe their loyalty? Can they be a bridge?

   Homework/written tasks:

   What will the mountain people no longer be able to say each other – e.g. song, lullaby, love letter (see example in resources).

   Describe two events in the days leading up to the banning that did not get shown on the television news.

Spend some time getting the shape of the tools right

The pupils could make a list of mountain words in their groups for the narrator to use

Groups may need to decide how to convey that two languages are being spoken

Point out that there needs to be a consistent convention e.g. both languages could be English as long as they are clear which characters do and do not understand each other.

Lesson 6: Pupils' Responses

Notes

These are responses from pupils who have worked on the scheme before

1. Teacher has ready on the board some questions or statements raised by students about *Mountain Language*.

   'Whatever happened to innocent until proven guilty?'

   'It's just wrong.'

   'In a time of fear you betray your friends.'

2. Teacher says: 'Somewhere on the outskirts of the city there is a particular wall. On this wall people write/tell the news/information that doesn't get onto the television news. With your group, create this wall on sugar paper. The people have a name for this wall. Decide with your group what they call it.'

   Pupils create and then view each other's walls.

3. Teacher says: 'Imagine you are a soldier in the army of the capital. One of your regular duties is to clean the words off the wall

   Write a monologue showing the soldier as s/he cleans the wall. A monologue is a speech in a play in which only one characters speaks.'

   The pupils write their monologues.

4. Teacher asks the class to work in pairs helping and guiding each other to perform their monologues.

   Show.

Lesson 7: What is art for?

1. Teacher reviews the past 5 lessons.
2. Teacher says – 'your commission is to devise, prepare and present a play entitled *what is art for?'*

Resources
Brief notes on Bond

Bond is considered to be one of the major living English playwrights, both in this country and abroad.

Edward Bond was born in London and educated in state schools until the age of 14. He was working in a factory when he became a member of the Writer's Group at the Royal Court Theatre.

His first plays, *The Pope's Wedding* (1962) and *Saved* (1965), were staged at the Royal Court Theatre. Censorship closed several of his plays after a couple of performances; they were judged to be too violent shocking, and immoral.

Though controversial, Bond has always had supporters and the critics and the public reversed their position on Bond after a revival of *Early Morning* less than a year after its original production in 1968.

Violence is seen as a tool Edward Bond uses to criticise society – never as an end in itself.

Introduction to the script extract from *Saved*

In this scene in Edward Bond's *Saved* a gang of young delinquents is depicted burning, urinating on and finally stoning a baby to death in its pram.

When this play first appeared at The Royal Court in 1965 it shocked and outraged many people. The play was censored – banned by the

Lord Chamberlain's office, a government office that examined and passed (or rejected) for performance any play for the English stage.

Nowadays this particular form of censorship of the theatre no longer exists, and it was the debate over *Saved* that helped bring the Lord Chamberlain's office to an end.

Pam is 23 and unmarried. She has a child. She has been living with Len, whom she now despises. Fred is 21; he is tired of Pam. Fred and several of his friends are in a park; they have been fishing. Pam enters, pushing a pram. Fred tells her he doesn't want to see her again, and after an argument Pam leaves her child with Fred. Len goes out after Pam.

Fred, Mike, Pete, Colin and Barry are left with the baby. They begin to fool about, pushing the pram from one to another, until their play becomes vicious. No one else is there to intervene, to keep control. The baby isn't their responsibility and Fred resents the idea that he is probably its father.

Pete pulls the pram from Colin, spins it round and pushes it violently at

Barry. Barry sidesteps and catches it by the handle as it goes past.

Brief Notes on Harold Pinter

Harold Pinter was born in Hackney, in London. He has taken part in many political campaigns involving the rights of freedoms of people around the world. He is a world famous playwright.

In 1949 he was fined by magistrates for refusing to do national service.

In December 1977, at the end of an introductory speech at the launch of a special exhibition of peace train photographs, Pinter said

'I'd like to finish here by reading something which I think is a remarkable piece of prose by Dario Fo, which he actually wrote quite recently and submitted to the Turkish press. '*Kurdistan lives. It burns in the mind of every single person of the 35 million people who were robbed of their identity and made into refugees in Turkey, Iraq and Europe.*'

In 1999, during the war in Kosova, Pinter condemned NATO's intervention and said it will 'only aggravate the misery and the horror and devastate the country.'

Mountain Language

One of the biggest influences on this play may have been Pinter's connection with Turkey. He was concerned about the abuses of human rights, the lack of freedom of speech and discrimination against the Kurds. The play was first performed in 1988 at the National Theatre, after he had written no plays for some time. It is about 25 minutes long and focuses on a brutal society which forbids a minority of its population to speak their own language. The action is set in a prison in an unspecified country. A group of women have come to see their husbands, fathers and sons, who are prisoners.

Script Extract from *Mountain Language*

'Officer: Now hear this. You are mountain people. You hear me? Your language is dead. It is forbidden. It is not permitted to speak your mountain language in this place. You cannot speak your language to your men. It is not permitted. Do you understand? You may not speak it. It is outlawed. You may only speak the language of the capital. That is the only language permitted in this place. You will be badly punished if you attempt to speak your mountain language in this place. This is a military decree. It is the law. Your language is forbidden. It is dead. No one is allowed to speak your language. Your language no longer exists. Any questions?' (p.10)

Two pieces of writing arising from class work on Mountain Language, written by the same year 10 girl. It seems to me that they demonstrate a student reaching for the understanding that comes from having stood in the shoes of both the city and the mountain people. Neither piece is without its contradictions. Her stance is not neutral.

A lullaby sung by a mother of the mountain people

Hush
Hush little child
Slowly drift away
There will be another day
When you learn our mountain ways
There will be another day
When you learn what your ancestors did
So lay down your sweet head
And close your eyelids
Let your mind carry you far away
To where the nightingales sing
Where you'll find
Life's such a beautiful thing
Life's like a rose
So sweet but misunderstood
Just because you prick your fingers on its thorns
Does not mean it's no good
Value the old
Who teach you with an open heart
Listen to what they have to say
And I promise we'll never be apart
Just dream of another day
When the whole family's sat by the fire
Praising you for your success
Giving you what your heart desires
So do no wrong
And give me all your love
And stay as faithful
As the pure and innocent dove
We will work all day
We will work all night
I will stand by you
I will always do you right
So do no wrong
Open your heart
So we will never be apart
Because it's love I bring
You sweet innocent thing
Let your mind carry you
To a place that is always mild
For I am your loving mother
And you are my precious child.

A description of a soldier character she was developing

My character
My character first appears in the play when he's standing in a building looking over his city. The way he is stood shows that he is a very powerful man that no one can hurt. The look on his face is devious and sly, he acts like a nice man, but he is just a 'petty tyrant'. The fact that he looks strong and unbeatable does not mean that he is. Inside, my character is insecure, he has had past dilemmas when he wanted to do something right but it went wrong. He is just that little boy inside.

He has one of his soldiers always around him. To him the soldier is a protector, somebody that protects him from harm or injury because he is scared.

The first line from my character reveals that he is cruel and vindictive, because the emphasis he puts in what he says shows that he is evil. It shows that he has no respect for the people he is talking about. I have to act to the audience and show them that underneath his entire armour he is like a soft-boiled egg. I have to show in his own way he is cruel but I also have to show that he is trying to hide something. The audience should feel a certain amount of power from him the first time he steps on stage.

Rosemond

The Crusades

A scheme of work preparing students for an examination

Introduction

This scheme of work was written for year 11 students, approaching the final unit of the OCR Drama GCSE Examination in 2003. This unit is called the Realisation Test, and it requires the students to devise an original performance in response to one of two stimuli sent by the board. In early 2003 the board sent an extract of *The Children's Crusade* by Paul Thompson and a black and white copy of the painting The Scream by Edvard Munch.

At the time that these arrived in the post, the news was full of the threats of the war against Iraq. The students' conversations, both formal and informal, showed that they were very aware and anxious about the war.

One boy's reaction stays with me. The drama room in which I usually teach overlooks a park. One day early in 2003, a helicopter flew over the park, disturbing my year 11 drama lesson. It circled more than once, and we could see it was not the usual police helicopter but one with army markings. A boy said;

> 'It's from the army – look, look'(the class gathered at the window)

> 'Miss (he continued), it's an army one – are we all going to die?'

He wasn't joking, he was scared. His question was both honest and exacting. In the immediate moment I provided reassurance – for the longer-term I provided the scheme below.

The students' work that came from this SoW was some of the best I have ever seen at GCSE. They were driven to make sense of and give voice to the world's terrors. I think the OCR Drama GCSE examiners that year gave classroom teachers a rich opportunity to work creatively with the needs and demands of the young people.

For this unit the students are required to work as devisers, designers, directors and performers. There is a six-week preparation period, followed by a two-day practical test. The areas of study prescribed by the board are:

> *Character and context*
> *Structure, Shaping and Plot*
> *Audience*
> *Defining performing space*
> *Improvisation*
> *Genre Style and Convention*
> *The Semiotics of Drama and Theatre*

NB: Each of the 'lessons' below took more than the usual hour allotted in the school timetable – most took three hours.

I have included the lesson on *The Scream* as it is qualitatively connected to the central tenor of the work.

Lesson 1: The Script

'What is the full cost of the passage?' (Scene 1, line 19/20)

1. Teacher explains that for this project the class will be working as performers, researchers, designers, devisers, directors, and begin as researchers – 'To be researchers we need to ask questions about the play, about the history of then, and about what is happening in the world now.'

   Teacher refers to the map of the world, and explains briefly the meaning of the word *crusades*, showing pictures of the early Christian crusades.

2. Teacher places the title question on board, followed by two others:

   a) How do the Cardinals and the Pope want the world to see them? (i.e. what is their 'appearance')

   b) What reality is the Old Crusader revealing?

   Whole class reads scene 1.

3. Teacher refers again to the questions and leads the class discussion with question a).

   During this discussion Teacher sketches a large red cross (like that worn by the Crusaders) on a large piece of paper. As the discussion progresses to question b) the teacher chooses something from the students'discussion to draw on another large piece of paper, e.g. a symbol for money.

   Teacher then sticks the two bits of paper together and cuts a simple neck-hole to form a paper tabard (this can also be done with wallpaper which has a fabric-like quality).

4. Teacher organises the students into small groups, as designers, asking them to:

   ■ Choose a design for the front and back of the tabard, revealing the reality (on the back) behind the appearance (on the front)

   ■ Choose a line from the scene to go on the front of the tabard e.g. 'we promise eternal life'.

   ■ Make the tabard

   Teacher gives each group a pair of bamboo sticks to form into a cross they can hang the tabard on to represent a crusader. The student can hold it as they might hold a banner.

5. Teacher counts down to a whole class depiction, with both the students and the scarecrow crusaders, illustrating the line:

   Our chief anxiety is for the liberation of the Lord's sepulchre in the Holy City.

6. Teacher directs a whole class depiction, building slowly through discussion, of students holding the banner crusaders to illustrate the line:

   The full cost.

Notes

Have script extracts ready (2)

Students in the role of the researcher/designer/ deviser. They are also studying context and semiotics

The word Crusade means, more or less, Cross Aid, referring to the Christian Cross

The school library should have some basic books.

Take care to address this with an historical 'cool strip'. How the teacher presents this potentially hot information is important. For example, the children may be Muslims, as many of those I teach are

Lesson 1: The Script (continued)

7. Teacher says: 'In order to help make connections between the present and the past we are going to imagine that we will be performing the play in 2 different venues. One of the venues will be a cultural centre in Basra, * in Iraq. What would be another suitable venue?'

    Homework – draft a letter to the United Nations head quarters giving a brief outline of what you think your play might be about and why you want to perform it there.

The week we were exploring what might be a suitable venue for showing a play, the incident over the tapestry occurred so I suggested that the United Nations headquarters in New York as a good place to stage this drama

* Suggested by colleague Guy Williams

Lesson 2: Interpreting the Script

Preparation –

–   Have the poem about parents written up on the board, and next to it have a comment column entitled 'how does the writer of this poem portray parents?'

—   Have the list of conventions ready to display

This lesson puts the students into the role of the performer/director. They are also studying style and convention

1. As the lesson begins Teacher asks the class to read the poem (see resources) and write comments in the column next to it.

2. Teacher conducts a warm up using breathing and voice exercises.

3. Circle. Teacher asks class members to read whole of scene 2, and discuss first impressions of the children and their families and friends.

4. Teacher asks – 'how should the humming be enacted?

    What's it for? What mood does it create?'

    Teacher takes one or two of the students' suggestions and tries them out with the whole class.

5. Teacher asks – 'how does the writer of this play portray parents? What mood and meaning does the writer want?'During this analysis Teacher refers to key lines.

6. Teacher divides the class into two groups. Group A is to express the view of parents portrayed by the playwright, group B that of the poem. They have 10 minutes to plan how to express the view, using action and a maximum of five words.

The aim here is to analyse what view of the families the writer is presenting, and whether as directors/ performers they would want to support this view or challenge it

7. As the groups show their work Teacher focuses the discussion on the meaning and execution.

8. Teacher asks: 'If you were directing this play, would you want to support the playwright's apparent portrayal of families and friends or challenge it?'

    Teacher conducts an example scene in the middle that challenges the obvious reading of the script. E.g. Mother (Jane) and Two Sons (Colin and Martin) – could be done with all 3 characters tight-lipped, or one sobbing, or in anger, or with Colin and Jane clinging to each other with Martin pulling them apart, or melodramatically,

In fact I did the alternative examples not in circle, but as a series of freezes, from which the class chose one to develop and show back. It was

Lesson 2: Interpreting the Script (continued)

Notes

or with the speed of farce, or with Jane giving the last of her food, or at the father's graveside, or with Jane wearing a large red cross and marching her children off. Teacher demonstrates how different ways of playing the scene can alter the meaning.

interesting that the pupils chose mostly to explain the parents' behaviour e.g. because they were single parents and/or on the point of starvation and had to push their children out into the world, or because they were deeply Christian

Homework – Teacher asks the class to create an illustrated plan for directing scene 2 that supports, explains or changes the playwright's portrayal of the children and their families.

Illustrated plan = a plan with actual examples of enactment of one or two moments

Before moving on to this next session, ensure that the class have grasped the idea of 'explain, support or challenge' the playwright's portrayal of parents/families'.

Lesson 3: Off Text

Leave in Peace, Come Home in Pieces

Notes

1. Circle. Teacher begins a discussion of reasons for performing at the United Nations headquarters, and asks: 'What is going on there at the moment?'

This section puts the students into the role of deviser and improviser. They are also studying structure, shaping and plot, audience, context and improvisation

2. Teacher asks the class to discuss in pairs: 'What would the Old Crusader say at UNHQ? What would we say?' and then report back. Teacher reads one or two of the homework pieces from lesson 1.

Do we, the teachers, know enough about the debate that was raging at the UN at that time, or now? Ask each other. Read the newspapers, research news pages on the web. Talk about our own understandings – or otherwise – don't be afraid that you don't know enough

3. Teacher organises the class into groups of three and asks them to expand the homework to produce a short scene that the group would like to perform at the UNHQ – alongside the showing of the scene, explain how it links to the play *The Children's Crusade.*

4. As the groups show their scenes to one another Teacher focuses the discussion on their possible impact on the intended audience, and what effect they would like their play to have on the audience at the UN, and helps them to be clear about what their plays are saying.

They could explain with e.g. narration or written titles

Student as performer

5. Teacher puts explanation of gest on the board, and explains to the class: 'We are now going to work on a moment from recent history that took place at the UNHQ.'

Gest = character's stance + actor's body language +ensemble stage picture working together to

95

Lesson 3: Off Text (continued)
Leave in Peace, Come Home in Pieces

Notes

Teacher explains the context, showing the picture of *Guernica* and explaining that it was painted by Picasso in response to the first ever air raid, on Guernica in Spain. Teacher makes it clear that it is an anti-war painting, drawing out examples of the anti-war symbolism of the painting. Teacher explains that a tapestry version of it was made, and hung in one of the public rooms in the UNHQ

juxtapose processes and demonstrate social political relationships, and moments of potential change.

6. Teacher begins to organise in role work. Tir as administrative/technical chief of staff at the UNHQ – pupils in role as technical/administrative staff. Teacher establishes pupil roles, e.g. one assistant chief of staff, cleaners, carpenters and handymen.

   Teacher countdown to depictions with thought tracking – the moments when
   - the tapestry was unwrapped
   - hung on the wall
   - the press came in to photograph it.

   Teacher explains that time has passed.

7. Tir: 'Colin Powell will be coming shortly to speak in this room to the press about the war on Iraq – his press secretary wants the Guernica tapestry covered up whilst he is speaking to the press – please could you ensure that this is done...'

   Teacher out of role – 'as the chief of staff turns to leave the room, what is in the minds of those who unwrapped and hung the tapestry?'

   Teacher spotlights for some to say what their character is thinking.

8. Teacher places question: '*How* will they carry out their orders?' Teacher asks class to prepare a small group scene concentrating on the gest of covering the tapestry. The groups show their work

10. Teacher places question: 'Would the people at the UNHQ have ears to hear and eyes to see the scenes that the class did previously? Is it a proper place for art?'

Lesson 4: The Script

Bread and blankets

1. Teacher recaps the work so far: the class has worked as deviser, designer, director and performer. They have studied character, context, audience, plot, shaping, improvisation, style and convention, and the semiotics of Drama.

   This could be the moment to choose the groups.

2. Teacher establishes where on the map of the world the children are now on their crusade and where they are heading. They are about to cross the threshold of the Alps.

3. Class reads scene 3 and Teacher asks class if they have any questions arising.

4. Teacher says: 'When they turn to cross the threshold of their home at the end of the scene, do the Farmer and his son they take the sack and blankets with them or leave them in the rain? Why?'

5. Class reads scene 4, up to the end of page 16.

   Teacher focuses the class on the physical conditions for the young crusaders.

   Teacher says: 'The old crusader has followed the children. They do not know he is there, but he is watching them, he will tell us what we should know.'

   Teacher asks the class to work in small groups. Using

   ■ the cloths, and their coats/bags and newspapers to represent the huddled groups of children

   ■ sugar paper to represent bread the children may or may not have

   ■ the banner crusaders (from lesson 1) to represent the Old Crusader who will tell us what we should know.

   The class are to recreate the scenes that Francis *sees* by the light of his torch. The only words are those spoken by the Old Crusader.

   Homework:

   Write the words of the Old Crusader.

You will need about 6 pieces of cloth to represent blankets and sugar paper, newspapers and a torch

This section puts the students into the role of deviser and improviser. They are also studying semiotics and character.

It helps if the pieces of cloth are of different sizes so that not all groups are equally provided for

If you can create a blackout you could use a torch to light the groups when they are presenting their work.

Session 5: The Script

Thousands of Impetuous Children ... It's a Recipe for Social Disorder

1. As the class come in Teacher gives them a newspaper clipping to read and discuss (see resources later).

2. Teacher outlines the dream sequences section of the script.

3. The class reads p.19-24.

   Teacher says: 'How will things end for the children on the crusade? What is their final threshold?

   Why has the exam board not given us the ending?'

   Discussion.

   Teacher moves discussion into next stage saying: 'We're going to explore the possible reasons.'

4. Teacher sets up a meeting – a table for Tir with torn up 'script' on it. The only visible piece of script is a fragment that says 'The Final Threshold'.

   Tir as assistant chief examiner, class in role as drama advisors, experts on drama in schools. The meeting begins with a depiction called 'the door of the meeting room has just slammed after one of the advisors has stormed out'

   Tir: 'For goodness sake, some people! What are we going to do now? We've got to have the thing ready for the printers by the end of today. How we can send it out incomplete? It's a silly play to choose altogether. It's bound to offend the Muslim community and I predict it's going to cause no end of trouble, although I'm not sure he should have torn it up like that.'

   Teacher encourages class to participate and holds the position that a solution has to be found and quickly.

5. Teacher out of role tells the class that they have to create either

   ■ the ending that was torn up

   or

   ■ one that the advisors create in its place.

   They must begin by deciding together, as a class,

   ■ where the scene takes place:

   E.g. in the doorway of a home the children left? At the seashore as the children wait for the sea to divide? By the city walls of Jerusalem (as a group of children there wait for the child crusaders who don't turn up)?

   They must decide exactly what that threshold is – e.g. sea, wall, doorway, and use paper to represent that threshold. Teacher asks: 'What could be written or drawn on it? Where would you place the figure of the Old Crusader?'

5. The groups show their devised scene that takes place on that threshold.

Notes

This section puts the students into the role of deviser and improviser and performer. They are also studying structure, shaping, plot and defining performing space

I don't think the class particularly need to read the dream sequence – it's partly a question of where you want to invest time

Lesson 6: Picture

The Scream

1. Teacher focuses class on the picture and says – 'What do you notice? The figure is on a bridge, turning away from the water. What are the qualities of that water?'

2. Teacher organises the class into groups and distributes current newspapers, from which they select and cut pictures and words to lay out and stick to sugar paper

3. When the collages are completed, the groups view and comment on each other's work.

4. Teacher asks the groups to create two depictions, which, together with the images on the sugar paper, answer the question: What are the qualities of that water?

5. Teacher asks the class to demonstrate the depictions simultaneously, and then to link the two depictions with movement and sound. When ready, Teacher asks one or two groups to demonstrate, and focuses the class on the semiotics of the work.

6. Teacher asks the groups to build on what they have created and to devise a movement and sound piece that answers this question: 'What needs to happen to stop the figure on the bridge screaming?' When ready, the groups show their work.

   Homework – revisiting the questions (see resources)

Notes

You will need newspapers featuring words/pictures of our world now

When war was declared on Iraq many of the students and staff from our school joined a local demonstration against the war. The preparation for it and the demonstration itself took place while we were working on this scheme

I included newspaper clippings of reports describing how some areas were planning to mount police outside schools to prevent students from joining demonstrations against the war

Lesson 7: The start of the two-day test

Group planning

1. Teacher: 'Imagine that as part of a peace building programme you will be taking your plays to perform in Basra.'

2. Teacher reads out extract from Dear Raed (see resources).

3. Teacher and class discuss – 'Looking back over the work of the past 6 weeks, what are the main questions/concerns you want to approach?'

4. Teacher organises the class into groups and asks them to plan a starting point for their piece.

Notes

Check they know that Basra is in Iraq

Choose an extract to read – the point is to show the physical conditions in Basra

You could revisit each lesson's questions (see resources)

Resources

Have a map of the world so you can trace the journey of earlier crusades, the children's crusade, and key countries in the Middle East.

You will need a picture of Picasso's *Guernica*.

You will need a copy of *The Children's Crusade* or a copy of the stimulus paper from OCR.

You will need about six pieces of cloth of different sizes.

You might also want

- sugar paper and/or ends of rolls of wall paper (woodchip has a nice fabric-like quality,
- bamboo sticks
- images of crusaders
- images of e.g. Iraq, Palestine

Newspaper clippings – these should reflect the news at the time of teaching the scheme of work.

Poem

If they hear a child crying
Only one thought runs through their mind
Is she mine?
Is he mine?
They stand up and search with their eyes
They spot their child playing, laughing in the pool
They smile to themselves, sit back down
And continue to read.
They'll always be there when you're doing your homework,
Stuck on no. 24
They come over
Do you need help? Yeah.
They cook your food
Help you look after your pets
And buy you things that you want
But don't need.
They'll stand up for you in any argument
Always take your side
And help you in any problems
They encourage you in any hobby
Playing an instrument, reading a book
Cooking a meal, riding a bike
They'll support you in life and
Whatever career you choose
They'll love you always
And we'll love them
Do you know what these magical things
I've been talking about are?
They're called
PARENTS
A. R. (aged 10)

Homework for Lesson 6

Here are some of the questions you have been asked over the past few weeks:
What is the full cost of the passage?
How does the writer of this play portray parents?
What would the Old Crusader say at UNHQ ? What would we say? Would the people at the UNHQ have ears to hear and eyes to see?
Where is the final threshold?
What are the qualities of that water?
What needs to happen to stop the figure on the bridge screaming?
On a separate sheet, compile your own list of questions or notes that could help you devise a play based on *The Children's Crusade* and/or *The Scream.*

The following is an extract from the web diary entitled:

Where is Raed?

22/3

4:30pm

Half an hour ago the oil filled trenches were put on fire. First watching Al-jazeera they said that these were the places that got hit by bombs from an air raid a few minutes earlier but when I went up to the roof to take a look I saw that there were too many of them, we heard only three explosions. I took pictures of the nearest. My cousin came and told me he saw police cars standing by one and setting it on fire. Now you can see the columns of smoke all over the city.

Today the third in the war, we had quite a number of attacks during daytime. Some without air-raid sirens. They probably just gave up on being able to be on time to sound the sirens. Last night, after waves after waves of attacks, they would sound the all-clear siren only to start another raid siren 30 minutes later.

The images we saw on TV last night (not Iraqi, jazeera-BBC-Arabia) were terrible. The whole city looked as if it were on fire. The only thing I could think of was 'why does this have to happen to Baghdad.' As one of the buildings I really love went up in a huge explosion I was close to tears.

Today my father and brother went out to see what happening in the city, they say that it does look that the hits were very precise but when the missiles and bombs explode they wreak havoc in the neighbourhood where they fall. Houses near Al-Salam palace (where the minister Sahaf took journalist) have had all their windows broken, doors blown in and in one case a roof has caved in. I guess that is what is called 'collateral damage' and that makes it OK?

We worry about daytime bombing and the next round of attacks tonight with the added extra of the smoke screen in our skies.

Guernica

A scheme of work based on an incident at the United Nations concerning a tapestry of Picasso's painting *Guernica*

Introduction

This scheme of work developed from *The Crusades* scheme, which I originally designed for a year 11 class. We were exploring what might be a suitable venue for showing a play they were devising just when the incident concerning the tapestry occurred, so I suggested that the United Nations headquarters in New York might be a good place to stage it. This notion inspired the Guernica SoW, which I wrote for year 10 students, for a workshop for teachers at an NATD conference, and a workshop for teachers in Novi Sad.

On 27 January, 2003, in the run up to the United States war on Iraq, officials at the New York headquarters of the United Nations hung a blue curtain over a tapestry reproduction of Picasso's *Guernica*, which hung at the entrance to the Security Council. This setting is often used by diplomats and others to make statements to the press. It seems that officials thought it would be inappropriate for Colin Powell, then US Secretary of State, to speak about the war on Iraq with Picasso's protest against the inhumanity of war as his backdrop. *Guernica* is a large mural, painted by Picasso to commemorate the first aerial bombardment of a civilian population. German and Italian squadrons obliterated the ancient Basque town of 5,000 inhabitants on April 26, 1937. *Guernica* has justifiably been held to be one of the masterpieces of modern art.

Lesson 1: Before

Notes

In advance teacher sets up two notice boards:

- One with 'outside' info to support the drama e.g. world events, information regarding the UN, a map of the world
- The other for the staff meeting room.

  Teacher should also:

- Arrange pictures of the inauguration of the UN in the centre of the circle, with a sheet saying 1945 at their centre. Underneath the sheet saying 1945, put another that says 'then and now'. Cover all these up so they do not distract from the business of starting a lesson.

- Have *For Now* (see resources) ready for display, with explanations of tendered and rendered.

  As the class enters the room music is playing, the outside notice board is there for them to look at.

Music – quietly upbeat. Music helps a class to settle – it can introduce the lesson, suggest a mood, ease the interval between those who arrive first and last, reassure a group that is new to each other, and signal the start of a lesson when it is turned off

1. Introduction: teacher reads *For Now* (see resources).

2. Teacher reveals pictures of inauguration of UN, gives some background information, and encourages questions from the class.

3. Teacher asks the class to prepare a depiction in groups with the caption:

   What should this place be like?

   As the groups show back, Teacher asks class to reflect on what is seen and what is meant.

   Teacher scribes what the class is saying.

   Day 1

4. Teacher explains that we are now moving forward in time: 'Quite some time. We are going to be working in role as people who work at the UN headquarters in New York.

Evoke 'now and then'

Theme of covering and uncovering is introduced

Whilst scribing, the teacher listens out for, notes, and *marks* what the place is like. *Marking* might mean emphasising certain words, pausing, questioning (not interrogative questioning but reflective questioning such as 'I wonder why...')

Each one of you is a member of the technical and administrative arts team. You are the team that is expert in and takes care of the works of art that the world has given to the UN.' Teacher shows pictures of some of the works of art for which they are responsible.

I found information in books in the school library. There is also information on the UN website

Lesson 1: Before (continued)

5. The class begins to create the staff. Teacher introduces: 'This is the room where the staff often meets – this is the staff notice board' – Teacher points out things from the notice board -in particular the agenda for the special staff briefing – 'what else might there be on the notice board and in the room?'Class compiles a list or quick map drawn by teacher.

See resources for the agenda for the special staff briefing – it helps to indicate the jobs they might do, and guide the class in the direction of these jobs. Ensure that the jobs chosen will enable the participants to participate in the hanging and then the covering

6. Teacher organises the class into a sequence of groupings to create a sequence of artefacts. As one artefact is completed teacher introduces the next one, questioning and developing the pupils as they work around the room

To begin with, pupils work in pairs creating items they attach to the notice board. As they come and attach them, teacher asks what kind of work they do, referring to the Agenda, and perhaps the works of art at the UN. In this way Teacher organises the class into groups, which sketch or create artefacts for the particular workshop or room in which they work in the UN headquarters. These should demonstrate something of the nature of their work or specialism, and perhaps indicate whether they take care of a particular work of art. In this way the class create their workrooms and their roles, as well as their working groups. They begin to establish working patterns and practices.

Class stop to take stock of what has been established so far.

7. Teacher asks each individual to create security passes for their roles. 'These passes are shown as you enter the building each morning. They are also the electronic keys to your workrooms. What personal item is on the back of your pass?' e.g. a photograph of someone they care about tucked into the back, or a personal motto, or a shopping list.

Try to keep the security guard *represented* and not acted by a pupil, for two reasons:

a) so that the participants continue to work in/on their own role

8. Teacher asks the class to devise pair improvisations of everyday conversations between the two workers and the (representation of) the security guard as the workers come into the headquarters each day.

b) to avoid stereotyped guards

c) to explore the nature of the operant paradigm at this place of work – we are moving from what it should be to what it is. e.g. guard as man, guard as machine

Teacher raises the question of how to represent the security guard? Coat on a coat hanger? Hat on a chair? The pairs decide how to demonstrate the guard.

Stated aim to class – keep the improvisation ordinary and everyday, to show something of what it's like to work in this place

As the work is shown, teacher pays attention to nuances of body language in order to tease out the power relationships that reveal the dominant paradigm.

Paradigm = organising principle that governs perception. See *The Fight for Drama – The Fight for Education*

Lesson 2: Later that day

Notes

1. As the lesson begins, teacher ensures that all can see the 'email' message sent to each member of the staff: Please ensure that you are fully prepared for the briefing this afternoon.
Please be ready to report back on the preparations you have made for the delivery of the Rockefeller Tapestry, and raise any queries or concerns you may have. Please let me know if any staff wish to bring family/children/spouses to the reception.

   Teacher organises the class into their workroom groups to prepare for the report back that they will make in role, and places this question: 'how do these people, in this special place, where the nations of the world unite, to speak the language of peace, demonstrate that they are worthy stewards of world treasures?'

2. Teacher-in-role convenes the Special Staff Briefing in the staff room, asking the class in role to report back and raise concerns. Teacher works in role as Assistant Chief Co-ordinator of the team. If necessary, during the meeting Tir stresses that the eyes of the world are on them, this is high stakes, and outlines the main points about the painting *Guernica*, its history, and the Rockefeller tapestry. (Towards the end of the meeting Tir asks for the reports to be typed up and submitted for the departmental progress portfolio.)

3. Out of role, teacher shows the class Picasso's Guernica – private reflection, perhaps personal notes.

4. Teacher counts down to the following whole class depictions with spotlighting:
   - ■ When the tapestry is unwrapped
   - ■ When the tapestry is hung on the wall
   - ■ When the press come in to photograph it
   - ■ During the reception

   Teacher brings the final depiction into action for a whole class spontaneous improvisation.

Notes column:

This prefigures the next staff meeting.

Have the picture of Guernica concealed and ready for display

Have email on display so all can see it.

For this section textbooks/notes on the care and maintenance of works of art, fabrics etc. are useful

Uncover

When I worked with the year 11 students I found that they took a quick and direct relationship to the painting. I simply held it and showed it to them. With the teachers I felt that the approach should be slowed down, as many of them would already know about the painting

Spotlighting: whole class in role but are in individualised depictions (as though in a bubble). This enables them to relate directly to the content through the teacher's voice and to hear one another's comments in reflective mode, rather than channelled through each other's roles/characters. Teacher indicates which individuals should speak, one at a time.

Lesson 2: Later that day (continued)

Notes

5. Teacher counts down to individual depictions: 'Later that evening, as they take off their shoes, the staff remember something they heard a child say in response to Guernica, either at the reception, or later at home.' Spotlight.

Could use torches or candles to set the atmosphere

NB: taking off shoes = uncovering – uncovering feet can have a particular resonance.

6. Teacher says: 'Time passes and times change. In some ways it is as though the world has turned, in others it is no more time than it takes for the eyelid to cover and then uncover the eye. The staff are back in their staff room. The Assistant Chief Co-ordinator has called another meeting.

    Outside the door of the staff room the Assistant Chief Co-ordinator is talking. The chatter in the staff room dies down as they realise that the conversation outside the door is getting heated. These are the words that they hear.

    Yes, I know, I know …. No there's nothing I can do, it's in the hands of security. No, I'm afraid I don't have time to tell them; you'll have to tell them – quick as you can if you please.'

    If possible, time things so that this comes just before a break.

Quite some time passed between the hanging of the tapestry and it being covered up. I wanted the class to create an investment in the care of the tapestry, so have glossed over the passage of time.

Lesson 3: Still Day 2

Notes

1. As the class come into the room encourage them to look at the notice boards with additions. Make sure they know who Colin Powell and John Negroponte were (see resources).

2. Teacher says:

    'Let us now return to that conversation outside the door.' Teacher asks for a volunteer to be the person that the Assistant Chief Co-ordinator is speaking to.

    'Here is the beginning of the conversation the staff didn't hear.'

    Teacher-in-role (outside 'staff room door', to volunteer) 'Colin Powell or John Negroponte, we're not sure who yet, will be coming shortly to speak to the press about the war on Iraq – their press staff want the Guernica tapestry covered up whilst they are speaking to the press – please could you ensure that this is done... Yes, I know, I know... No there's nothing I can do, it's in the hands of security. No, I'm afraid I don't have time to tell them, you'll have to tell them – quick as you can if you please.'

Add the coffee shop notice and the security notice to the staff notice board

Add information regarding Colin Powell and John Negroponte to the 'outside' notice board. This can be found on the web on news sites

3. Whole class role-play – the volunteer enters the staff room and tells the staff.

    At a suitable point teacher asks role-play to freeze and asks 'what is in the minds of those who unwrapped and hung the tapestry?' Role-play continues if appropriate.

    Teacher judges when to bring the role-play to a close.

I gave the groups a blue cloth to use

Much of what happens in the small groups will stem from the whole class role-play. It is not unusual for people to refuse to cover the tapestry. The question

Lesson 3: Still Day 2 (continued)

Notes

then is, what will happen to their job?

Gest = character's stance + actor's body language +ensemble stage picture working together to juxtapose processes and demonstrate social political relationships, and moments of potential change

4. Teacher asks class to prepare small group scenes that show how the workers will carry out their orders and concentrate on the gest of covering the tapestry. Perhaps use slow motion – focus on actions of the hands in relation to the body and the head.

    As the groups show their work Teacher reflects in detail.

5. Teacher says: 'As Powell speaks to the world we know the picture is covered, but is it silenced? The hand that signed the cover up of the Contras holds the hand that signed the cover up of My Lai and together they cover Guernica. Beneath the blue cover the picture cries out. What does it say?'

6. Teacher asks the class to each take one part of the picture (e.g. the bull, the light, the mother and child, the two women) and build up a sound collage.

Lesson 4: The Last Day

Notes

In one version of this scheme I closed the UN headquarters to the staff – they had refused to cover up the tapestry and so their passes were rendered invalid.

1. Teacher and class recap the key events of the previous lessons.

2. Teacher asks the class to work in groups to prepare a scene: 'As the staff come into work this time, how do they show their passes to the security guard. How do they walk past the (now uncovered) tapestry?'

    As the groups show their work, teacher reflects on the how.

3. Teacher asks the class to return to exercise 3 in lesson 1: 'What *is* this building like?'

Resources
For Now

Now the questions begin
Now the bombing has stopped
For now
There are those who seek justice and call for accounts to be rendered
There are those who seek peace and call for amounts to be tendered.

- small pieces of paper or card
- picture of *Guernica* – I ordered this from a web address – there are several of them
- pens/pencils
- sugar paper
- scissors
- wall paper
- coat hangers

The resources below were gathered from school library books and from the web. It was fairly easy to find most things using a search engine.

- picture of inauguration of UN
- universal Declaration of Human Rights
- descriptions of the works of art.
- information on John Negroponte – US Ambassador to UN
- information on Colin Powell – US Secretary of State

Resources for Staff Notice board

Day 1
Inclement weather

During inclement weather, such as a severe snowstorm, flooding or hurricane, the Headquarters building will normally remain open, with essential services arranged by the relevant departments and offices. If the weather disrupts normal commuting patterns, a staff member should inform his or her supervisor accordingly. Supervisors should exercise flexibility and understanding in such circumstances. Unless the UN buildings are officially declared 'closed', staff absences will be charged to compensatory time-off balances or annual leave. Absences during scheduled work time of less than two hours need not be recorded.

Day 2

The UN premises will be officially declared closed only if there is a threat to the security and safety of staff or the building. Under these circumstances, an announcement will be placed on the UNHQ Information Website and on the Hotline (212) 963-9510. In such cases, staff absences will be recorded as authorised in compliance with paragraph 2.2 of ST/AI/1999/13, dated 9 November 1999.

Coffee Shop
The Coffee Shop, located in the Public Concourse, is closed indefinitely till further notice.
Security Pass:

Security Section	Sec 0085-03
	Section: technical and administrative
	Division: arts
Staff	
	Name:
	Number:

Agenda for Special Staff Briefing
Rockefeller Tapestry
- Arrival, unpacking
- Hanging
- Tapestry care check
- Veiling
- Lighting
- Sound
- Unveiling
- Staff and Delegates' Reception
- Press

The Voices that Could Speak from *Guernica*:
The bull
Mother and child
The Severed Head
The horse
The flower
The two women
The figure with raised arms
The light

Email:

Please ensure that you are fully prepared for the briefing this afternoon. Please be ready to report back on the preparations you have made and raise any queries or concerns you may have. Please let me know if any of you wish to bring family, children or spouses to the reception

Gilgamesh

A scheme of work based on the ancient epic of King Gilgamesh

Introduction

I first began working from this story in preparation for a workshop with teachers in Gjilan, Kosova in February 2005. I began with the episode in the cedar forest. For the most part, however, this scheme shaped the beginning of a GCSE Expressive Arts course. It was designed to establish a creative, expressive stance, both with pupils who were starting out on their GCSE years in school, and for the three teachers who would be working together in this way for the first time. It contains a curriculum contents table, and at the end of the scheme are some notes made whilst I was teaching it.

The GCSE Expressive Arts (OCR) syllabus requires students to:

Respond to a stimulus provided by the teacher.

Work collaboratively in a group reflecting the Areas of Study (atmosphere

Narrative, symbol, genre, subject, shape).

Make a plan and refine ideas; consider alternatives and available resources; make appropriate choices.

Work in at least two art forms, exploring, experimenting and developing skills.

Apply appropriate skills, processes and/or techniques.

Consider genre and style and make the most appropriate selection for art forms used.

Understand something of the cultural and historical influences on the art forms chosen.

Refer to, evaluate and make connections with works seen, heard or experienced within the art forms chosen.

Identify his or her individual contribution.

Communicate using relevant skills and with a clear sense of intended audience.

Reflect critically on the activities undertaken.(OCR p.13)

The Specification aims for the teacher of Expressive Arts to provide opportunities for active participation in the arts in order to

'Stimulate, encourage and sustain' pupils' confidence, as well as 'foster curiosity, ingenuity and imagination in the shaping of ideas, experiences and feelings' (OCR p.10)

This scheme of work also intended to demonstrate the creative process for the teachers. This was structured in two ways:

– The music and dance teachers read and discussed the drama scheme, which contained developmental questions for Music and Dance.

– The dance teacher and drama teachers were able to work alongside each other, watching and participating in each other's lessons, and both the dance and the drama teachers were in the music teacher's lesson watching and participating.

At the time I was planning this course I was reading *Gilgamesh – A new English Version* by Stephen Mitchell and re-reading Robin Dunbar's *The Human Story*. I was struck by these two sentences from Dunbar's book:

> *'teaching is extremely rare in the animal kingdom'* (Dunbar 2005 p.159).

> *'the key to teaching in humans is intentionality'* (*ibid* p. 160).

It seemed to me that the 'matter' of this story was a development of the 'matter' of the *The Facility*. When juxtaposed with both the content and the context of the story of *Gilgamesh*, Dunbar's observations set me thinking again about how it is that we have learnt to be human – how we move and how we see others move, the sounds we make and how we hear the sounds others make, how we see ourselves and how we see others, how we understand our individual being and how we understand our social being – how we are able to know what another human is thinking and feeling.

For many years I have integrated drama with music and sequenced movement, as both a stimulus and a framework for creativity in Drama lessons. Working in the inner city with pupils from around the globe and across classes and cultures, I have had to find ways of working that were accessible and inclusive and that enabled me to conduct whole class lessons. I found that music and expressive movement enhanced the educational Drama process. The move towards expressive arts is a logical development.

I began trying out ideas with my year 9 classes in Drama lessons, exploring both the combination of the art forms and the content. As ever, the children guided me in what it is they need to know. I worked further on the scheme for the 2005 NATD conference.

Content	The perception of self in relation to others
	The actions of self in relation to others
	How we understand our individual being and how we understand our social being
	Human bonding
	(Stewardship)
Concepts	Human organisation
	Innocence
	Becoming Human
	Change/History/Cause
Skills	
1 Thinking	*Generating ideas through exercising the creative imagination.*
	Fostering curiosity, ingenuity, and imagination in the shaping of ideas, experiences and feelings
	Providing direct experience of the creative process.
	Working collaboratively in a group
2 Accessing knowledge and communicating understanding	*Stimulating, encouraging and sustaining candidates' confidence providing opportunities for active participation in the arts, paying particular attention to atmosphere, narrative, and symbol*
	Working collaboratively in a group
3 Physical and sensorimotor	*The shaping of ideas* through dance, movement, music, and use of objects
Learning Material	The legend of Gilgamesh – the transformation of human society from hunter-gatherers to city dwellers, through the medium of the first recorded story
	Expressive Arts forms

Note: Pupil – a person taught by another

(Originally from the Latin pupa meaning 'girl' or 'doll'. When first used in English it meant 'orphan' or 'ward'). The same Latin root applies to the other meaning of pupil, i.e. the centre of the eye. It 'acquired its English meaning from the phenomenon whereby one can see a tiny reflected image of oneself in another person's eyes.' *Concise OED* p.1166

Part 1: The First Story Ever Read
(Context inside and outside the story)

1. Teacher introduces the story of Gilgamesh:

    'This is a story that disappeared for over 3000 years – hidden beneath the mounds of Nineveh – the sands of time – waiting patiently for those with eyes to see and minds to understand – until 150 years ago, when fragments of it were found. This story, the first story ever to be written, and so, I'm guessing, the first story ever to be read, is written on clay tablets (teacher shows mock up of a clay tablet).

    'When it was first discovered no one knew how to read it – can you imagine that? Written 3000 years ago and no one knew how to read it? So what did they do? They brought it back to the British Museum. Where it waited... for 25 years. Until one clever code breaker, an expert in reading, suddenly leapt up from his desk one day in 1872, tore off his jacket and waved a tablet in the air and pranced around the room in wild excitement. He had found out how to decipher it. And so the story was read again – and yet, you know, there are still bits of it missing – bits of it that we can only guess at.'

    (Teacher pulls out from below the yellow cloth the first fragment of the story).

    'This story begins close to the beginning of (pause) civilisation – a time when the hunter gathers were abandoning their nomadic patterns and settling – there are many rumours as to why we settled – why we left the forests and the plains, why we stopped our following the great herds. Some put it down to the first stirring of the mighty festival, and there is evidence for that, others that the course of the flood plains altered, the climate changed and we gathered at the river – two rivers in fact that became the arms that rocked the cradle of (pause) civilisation – we built our new ways on the land between two rivers – Mesopotamia – what we now have come to call Iraq.'

    Teacher shows where Iraq is on the world map.

2. Teacher reads the first story extract, the description of Gilgamesh – p.71 from *'surpassing'* to *'and one third human'*

3. Teacher places question: 'what would it be like to be ruled by Gilgamesh?' for the class to discuss.

4. Teacher pulls the next extract from beneath the 'sands' and reads p.72 from *'who is like Gilgamesh'* to *'is this how you want your king to rule?'*

5. Teacher asks class to work in small groups to create depictions of Gilgamesh as he goes about the city and places the title – *'the city in his possession he struts through it trampling its citizens like a wild bull.'*

    As the groups show their pieces, Teacher asks the class to say what kind of a city this is.

    As the lesson concludes, Teacher says: 'I wonder what shadow Gilgamesh casts?'

Notes
Area of Study:
Narrative

Words on board before lesson starts:
Gilgamesh
  Uruk
  Aruru
  Anu

Resources:
World map on display, time-line on display, CD, 'clay tablets'. I use the fragments of the story written out on one side of a page with images of clay tablets on the back of the paper, hidden beneath a yellow cloth.

Dance – The Tyrant King – what dances are the people **required** to do for him?

Music – The Tyrant King – What kinds of songs are the people **required** to create for him?

Commentary

As the context was established I made notes of responses from members of the class. I took the responses to see if they could be categorised according to implied form. Of course, many of them can fall into more than one category. The pupils' statements are also packed with content. In reply to the question 'What it would be like to be ruled by Gilgamesh?' the pupils said:

movement	sound	narrative	action	Character – demonstrating
He would trample all over people	He is very controlling	He will enslave people He will humiliate people. Things will get done.	People are scared in front of the king.	No respect for the people. He'll be 'trickish' – he'll persuade with sweet talk and be evil behind closed doors.

In reply to the question 'What kind of a city is this?' the pupils said:

movement	sound	narrative	action	Character – demonstrating
People can't look at their king. People offer up to their king. They have to kneel on the floor in fear.	There are frightened cries.	There are people who are illegal. People are scared of the consequences if they don't do as told.	People have to hide. People have to bow down to another human.	People are scared in front of the king.

Part 2: Apples for the picking
(Context in the story)

1. Teacher pulls the next extract from beneath the 'sands' and reads the description of the city, p. 70.

   Teacher says: 'It must have been quite something to have lived in one of the first ever cities – a whole new way of living – '*the palm trees, the gardens, the orchards.*' It must have been quite something to have been one of the first gardeners, one of the first arborists. I wonder what they were like, these first gardeners – what new knowledge they had gathered so that they could create these first gardens.'

   Class discussion of what the gardeners might have known.

2. Teacher uncovers the fruit: 'so from those qualities, this knowledge we, us humans, became skilled at growing apples – first found in Kazakhstan, not so far away from where our story is set, apples for the picking, where we want, when we want'.

   As the teacher talks she slices into some of the fruit and shows the seeds, colour and juiciness: 'They knew how to grow one of these (indicating fruit) from one of these (indicating seed).'

3. 'What would they have made sure was in their gardens?'

   As the class begin to make suggestions teacher begins to concretise them by asking them to list, on a piece of sugar paper, various features of a garden; and teacher begins to speak to the class as though they are

   - gardeners
   - tree workers – arborists

4. Teacher eases the class in to groups to design/ create gardens with paper on paper, allowing it to take the time it needs. Teacher circulates

   - making sure that the material constraints of growing plants and trees are born in mind
   - asking whether there is anything that they don't want Gilgamesh to know about them.
   - asking if that is reflected in the garden.
   - encouraging the pupils to use the design sheets and information on gardens.

Resources: 'clay tablets' beneath yellow cloth, garden design guides and craft materials. Also fruit and knife, covered. I use a shiny, silvery cloth to cover them and then use it again as the water. I use a mixture of real and plastic fruit. I use plastic fruit for two reasons:

– economy – it lasts and can be used several times

– you need some real fruit so that you can cut it and show seeds and the colour and the juiciness of it. Apples are good; pomegranates are wonderful for richness of colour and seeds

The contrast between the plastic and the real fruit is resonant of the boundary between what is real and what is fiction

I have noticed that as I uncover the fruit the class often comment on which of the fruits are real and which are not. There is an excitement and tension in their voices as they tell each other which are which.

The fruit knife lays a trail for later

The fruits (pomegranate? passion fruit?) also lay a trail, but a different one, one that may be traced towards Shamhat's initiation of Enkidu

Dance – As the gardeners move about their work how do they move?
What patterns do they make as they move around the gardens? How do their movement show us the nature of their work?

Music –
1. As the pupils enter the classroom *Strange Fruit* is playing – once the class are settled play it again. Try to avoid discussing it.
2. Teacher says: 'In the gardens of Uruk the gardeners sometimes sing quietly to themselves. What kind of songs do they sing?'

Lesson 3: The Shadows Show Us What They Know
(The actions of the self in relation to others)

Notes

Area of Study:
Atmosphere
Put on the board
– *If only the shadows
could show us what they
know*

1. Teacher says:

   'Gilgamesh will come to see your gardens – these lovely gardens that give us fruit and shade from the noonday sun. In this hot country, where the hot light of the sun beats down. One gardener will be chosen to show Gilgamesh around the garden. The group of gardeners should help that gardener plan what he will say to Gilgamesh.'

   Teacher counts down to:

   Depiction 1 – one gardener and one Gilgamesh.

   Depiction 2 – add in one shadow of Gilgamesh and one shadow of the gardener.

   Teacher gives title *If only the shadows could show us what they know.*

   Teacher counts down to

   Depiction 3 – what other shadows are there in the garden?

2. Teacher asks the class to bring depiction 3 to action for 10 seconds, all groups simultaneously, with dialogue and movement and places the question:

   'What truths can the shadows tell us?'

   The groups begin to develop this depiction to action into a scene.

2. Teacher interrupts the group work and plays track 9 for the class to listen to.

   Teacher asks: 'what part of your scene could you do to this music? Allow the music to give purpose to your movement.'

   Groups continue rehearsing.

CD
The Long Journey Home
– Peter Gabriel (5)

4. As the groups show their scenes, Teacher puts the truths on the flip chart.

   As the lesson concludes, Teacher recaps the atmosphere of the city from lesson 1 and the atmosphere of the gardens and finishes with: 'I wonder how the people will put up with such a king?'

Dance – The characters and their shadows: if the characters freeze, do the shadows interact? Can the shadows communicate with their characters?

Music – Songs/music that both hide and show the truth (codes, irony) – how could you create a song that both shows and hides the truth? NB: try not to be too literal – sometimes it's easy to make the truth a foregone conclusion, preventing any journey of discovery for the pupils.

Above: The gardener shows Gilgamesh the garden – the shadows are merely shadows.

Right: As the gardener guides Gilgamesh around the garden, the gardener's shadow strangles the sleeping shadow of the king.

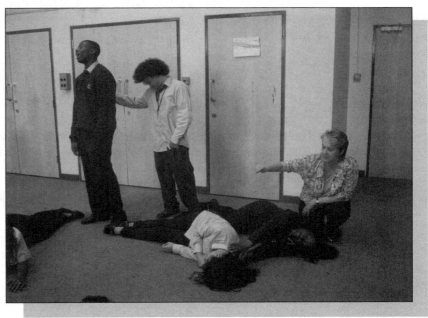

Lesson 4: The Mirror

(The perception of self in relation to others – what is it to be human?)

Symbol

Put on the board
Innocence

1. Teacher recaps the question from the last lesson and says that the people of Uruk cried out for the gods to save then from King Gilgamesh. The gods decided to create a match for Gilgamesh.

   Teacher asks for the definition of innocence, as in the innocence of a child.

   The 'we' refers to the pupils as both themselves and as gardeners

2. Teacher reads to the class, p. 73 to end of first paragraph on p.75. the description of Enkidu living 'free' and releasing animals.

3. Teacher places large sheet of shiny paper in centre of circle. 'We all know the value of water – we can visualise Enkidu – as Enkidu kneels by the water can he see himself in the water – can animals?' Class discussion.

   Animals can see reflected movement in shiny surfaces – but they do not know reflection, as humans can know them

   Teacher creates a depiction in the centre of the circle with some of the class as animals and one as Enkidu: 'The breeze stills and the pool becomes a mirror – the centre of the mind's eye – his image reaches out to him but can he see it? The breeze stirs again and there are many images.

   The answer given by the year 9 class, the first time I worked on this, was that he could be a god, a man or monster

   In his reflection is contained all that he could be – what is that he could be?' Class discussion.

4. Teacher organises group depictions – one person in each group is Enkidu and the others are his reflection – more than one can play his reflection. Teacher coaches the groups' depictions into actions: 'Enkidu is at the waterhole, with his reflection reaching out to him, encouraging him to be what he could be. At what moment does he, if ever, see his reflection? What happens to the water at that point? Will the reflections speak?'

   The groups develop their actions into rehearsed scenes.

   The class may need to practice mirror work.

   CD

   The Long Journey Home – Peter Gabriel

   Teacher asks groups to run their scenes simultaneously.

5. Teacher asks class to listen to track 15 and use this to show how Enkidu approaches the water hole, and the point at which the reflection appears.

   Rehearse and show. What have we learned?

Dance – What is the relationship between the reflections? (e.g.use of cannon)

Music – Sound collage of (atmosphere) Enkidu at the waterhole – include the animals, landscape and heat. How could we mark the moment when he sees himself? How can we create the water?

Commentary

The Bowl of Water

The dance teacher has watched the drama lesson, where Enkidu, the *human to be*, sees himself in the water.

In that drama lesson the class created a movement episode. It demonstrated:

a) What happens to the water when Enkidu first *sees* his own reflection

b) What possibilities for his future being are contained in the image in the water.

The class created highly focused pieces showing Enkidu amazed and confused, at times turning or running away from the waterhole yet still curious and driven to return to that place of disturbance. In their pieces they show how the water and the reflections combine to offer possibilities of being

- a beast
- a king
- a warrior
- a god
- a human being

In the lesson a silver cloth was used to signify water. One of the groups uses this cloth in their piece to

- flow like the water
- come between Enkidu and his reflection
- hover over Enkidu and his reflection
- be the robe of a king
- be the route taken by the sword of a warrior.

They allow themselves to let the music give purpose to their movement.

The dance teacher prepares the next lesson. She asks for a bowl of water. This is placed on the floor and the class gathers around the bowl. The dance teacher puts her hand in the water. She demonstrates the movement of the water.

What is to be seen in the movement of the water?

The water comprises countless tiny atoms (the individual)

The ripples coalesce, shatter, move together again (the group)

At times the water flows as one whole body (the class)

The dance teacher has choreographed a dance in which the class move, sequentially

- as one, in unison
- one after the other, in cannon
- individually,
- in groups, developing their drama pieces
- as a whole again except for one individual who meets his reflection at each turn.

Why does this work flow so well? Because two teachers are working together, watching each other's lessons, watching the class, watching the work, seeing the gains in the moment to moment unfolding of the lesson as it happens. – a spiral of mutual inspiration. As they create them for the class the teachers are creating zones of proximal development (Vygotsky) for each other.

Lesson 5: The Pupil in the Eye
(Human bonding)

1. Teacher recaps definition of innocence.

2. Teacher reads to the class p.75 – 76: Enkidu releases animals from traps, affecting the trapper's livelihood. The trapper's father advises him to talk to Gilgamesh. Teacher makes decision, depending on the class and the context, either to read or to tell in his/her own words the section in which Gilgamesh advises the trapper to ask a priestess to initiate Enkidu into society, thus removing him from his animal state. Ditto the section in which this advice is carried out, p.78- 81.

Put on the board
Innocence
Trapper
Shamhat.

Have a prop knife ready

3. Teacher places silver cloth in centre of circle, and says: 'Imagine at the water hole one day – Enkidu – fascinated by his reflection, as he plays with his hair in his image in the water he becomes aware of another combing her hair beside him and their movements echo each other's. He turns – their eyes meet.

4. 'And so the trapper and the priestess caught Enkidu, and the wild man became human,' Teacher pauses for discussion: 'Would he have changed so willingly? Why? NB: p.80 what about that 'longing for a true friend?'

5. Teacher says: 'So Shamhat takes Enkidu into Uruk.'

Teacher counts down to a whole class depiction to action – 'Enkidu enters Uruk. How does the city affect him?'Teacher asks class to repeat and refine, focusing on the sounds of the city and Enkidu's reaction.

6. Circle. Teacher asks: 'What do you think the gardeners would like Enkidu to learn about as he sees these gardens for the first time?' Discussion. Teacher asks volunteers to create a depiction in circle: the gardeners prepare for Enkidu's visit.

The class are now in the position of teaching the knowledge they have acquired

'As the gardeners prepare, so Enkidu is made ready for the fruits of civilisation. The priestess's servant is preparing him for city life.'

Teacher-in-role as priestess's servant – places a chair in a different part of the circle and asks for a volunteer to be Enkidu or, depending on the class, creates a representation of Enkidu.

Not Teacher-in-role as the priestess – this needs to be 'grey' role – the priestess would be too high status and too full of the content of the lesson – the class need to come to the content through the garden and through Enkidu

7. Once the depiction is ready, Teacher says: 'As they work in their gardens the gardeners hear a loud shouting – they stop and look towards the temple where the shouting is coming from.' Pupil depiction.

'This is what they can hear, but cannot see'.

Tir with Enkidu says: 'No-one can wander around this city with their face all covered up, we must be able to see you properly, you must cut your hair – priestesses orders!' Tir wields prop knife and mimes slicing Enkidu's hair. 'And so, hair cut, newly bathed and robed Enkidu is shown around the gardens of Uruk. I wonder how he feels as he enters the garden.' Teacher pauses so the class can respond. Teacher places Enkidu in the gardeners' depiction in the circle and asks the pupils to bring it to life.

8. Teacher asks class a reflection question to discuss in groups and report back on: 'What is it that Enkidu is learning? How do the gardeners behave towards him?'

Commentary

It is important for the teacher to understand that it is possible that women had a high status role in some early societies that was sexual, one which is difficult for us to grasp in our times. One theory is that the early matriarchal societies viewed sex as the male's opportunity to connect to the earth and to nature and that women were leaders, and privy to special knowledge, e.g. about medicine and health, food, conception, birth. In the story of *Gilgamesh* we seem to see this worldview in transition so the role of the priestess has become separated from the seat of political power. Nevertheless, it is an honoured position. It is likely, however, that our class may find this hard to grasp and might misinterpret it.

The moment of the meeting between Shamhat and Gilgamesh could be enacted as a reprise of the reflection/mirror work from lesson 4.

At this stage of the SoW the music and dance teachers were encouraged to move the next two sections of the story themselves. The dance teacher created the meeting between Enkidu and Gilgamesh, the fight between them and the resolution of the fight in which they become close friends and 'brothers'.

The music teacher took the episode in which Enkidu and Gilgamesh travel to vanquish Humbaba, the guardian of the sacred cedar forest, which they decimate so that Gilgamesh can build temples with the wood.

There is also a drama version of this episode.

Lesson 6: The Destruction of the Cedar Forest

Symbol

1. Teacher sets out objects made from wood in front of the class. Teacher narrates:

    'In ancient Uruk on the street of the cedar workers where craftsmen turn wood into wonders, King Gilgamesh and his brother Enkidu address the men.'

    TIR as Enkidu reading the speech on behalf of Gilgamesh – Gilgamesh can be signed by e.g. a red cloak draped over a chair.

    TIR as Enkidu says: 'Those men amongst you who love all that is good, who know the ways of the world of man, who know the value of this earth's riches, listen now as I read you the words of lord Gilgamesh.

    'We call on you to gather and march with us – we must travel triumphantly to the forest of the mighty Cedar – we must defeat the monster Humbaba, who threatens all that is human, who threatens the ways of just men and denies us the legacy of the gods, which is truly ours. We have fine temples to build and ships to sail – the progress of our great nation depends upon your mighty work and skills. We must harvest the riches of the cedar forest. Those men amongst you who have pride in our progress, and know, first hand, of the advances we have made, who care for legacy of craft we will leave, step forward.'

Resources:
– Objects which should signify key aspects of human culture – things that signify e.g. agriculture, family, domesticity/home, concealment, puzzles, skill, craft/art

– Paper and pens/pencils, scissors

– Information on the cedar tree and its uses (see resources)

– Extract from book p.124.

Lesson 6: The Destruction of the Cedar Forest (continued)

2. Teacher counts down to a depiction:

   'As they step forward, the carpenters and craftsmen hold out their hands to sign up, to make their mark.'

3. Tir as Enkidu 'reporting' to Gilgamesh:

   'See brother – the strong fingers that can bend and mould, confident hands who give shape to the song the wood sings, old scars from apprentice days when the chisel slipped, strong shoulders and calves which daily turn the lathe, clear skin from the steam of oil extraction, fine lines around eyes that know how to focus. Surely these men are true for our cause (he turns back to the men). You men, Lord Gilgamesh is satisfied. Prepare yourselves for our righteous journey.'

   Teacher says: 'In the workshops the tools and interrupted work lie waiting. The men must return to their workshops to prepare for their journey and shut up shop. What work do they put away for safe-keeping?'

4. Teacher asks the class to:

   – draw the piece of work that was interrupted
   – sketch and cut out one tool that they will carry with them to the cedar forest.

   As the class draw, teacher circulates information on the cedar tree and its uses.

5. Teacher asks the class to create a depiction of the thoughts of the men as they secure the door to their workshop. Spotlight and hear some of those thoughts.

6. Teacher says: 'And so with these thoughts the men travel the great journey to the cedar forest – the journey takes them a vast distance and across mountains and they must travel fast to keep pace with Gilgamesh and Enkidu. Finally, they come to the edge of the great cedar forest. They stop to listen – and for a while there is silence.

   Then they hear the sounds of one of the world's great forests. What is it they can hear?'

   The class build a sound collage:

   ■ list the sounds they can hear
   ■ in groups experiment in creating the sounds with whatever is to hand
   ■ bring together and Teacher orchestrates.

7. Teacher says: 'The men stand on the edge of the mighty cedar forest, listening to the sounds and peering in.' Teacher spotlights individuals asking: 'What can you see?'

8. Teacher says: 'And as they see these sights, another image begins to take shape, working its way into their consciousness – the shape of the monster Humbaba.'

   Teacher reads extract of the fight, p.124. The forest is devastated.

9. Teacher-in-role as Enkidu: 'Men, my brother and I thank you – we have defeated the monster Humbaba and now the free world of men can rejoice. Gilgamesh and I will return immediately to Uruk.

Lesson 6: The Destruction of the Cedar Forest (continued)

We will take this mightiest of all the cedars so that work on the temple door can begin at once. We leave you here to collect, grade and carve this precious wood.'

10. Teacher asks the class to prepare a depiction/action/ depiction in which the men begin their work. Teacher says: 'What is in their movement that tells us what us in their minds?'

   After the groups have been working for a while, Teacher interrupts the work and asks the groups to show, simultaneously, the depictions/ moments from the sequence. Teacher feeds back what she sees, noting signs of disturbance. Teacher feeds in new information: 'As the men pick up the wood or work on it, some are seen to discard it hastily (sign), moving quickly to another piece – others work on undisturbed.'

   Groups rehearse and show their scenes.

11. Teacher: 'And so this is how the work is done. In the evening the men gather round the fire. They are quiet.'

   Tir as man with a pipe in his/her hand;

   'I noticed you today – you threw away your carving – I saw you break it up (pause) I saw several of you, didn't I? (pause – burst out) look, I can't stay here, this place gives me the creeps'– Tir goes to throw the pipe on the fire and freezes.

   Teacher narrates: 'And as he hesitated there he remembered the words he had heard as he played the pipe.

   You have betrayed your legacy. You have broken the rules of the forest. Rule 1 – you must...

   And in fact he hadn't been the only one to hear these words as they worked.'

12. Teacher asks: 'What are these rules of the forest of which the wood speaks?'

   Whole class contributes as Teacher scribes.

13. Teacher says: 'When they are back in Uruk, when they have returned to the street of the cedar workers, will the men still have the ears to hear the song of the wood?'

   Depiction/action/ depiction.

14. Teacher says: 'In the place where the cedar forest was, the fallen trees are shadows of their former selves.'

Lesson 7: Devising

1. Teacher distributes Reflection and Response. Teacher asks the class to read it through in pairs and respond with a question and a memory of the work.

See resources

2. Teacher reads out letter from the Director of The Freedom Museum of Human Being, and says that the Director will be arriving very soon. Teacher asks if there are any questions to raise before the Director arrives, and asks the class if they have any idea what the exhibits might be in this museum.

See resources

3. Teacher-in-role as Director asks the class if they have any questions. Of course, whatever the students have 'supposed' will be in the museum turns out to be what the museum contains. The Director establishes that the class will work in groups to produce a presentation representing what people could learn from the story of Gilgamesh, to be presented in the Freedom Museum of Human Being.

4. The class begin to work in groups, planning, devising and rehearsing. They are given about 3 lessons to complete this process.

Resources

Research Task for Students

Information	Question
Climate Change	
The British Prime Minister has said climate change is 'probably long-term the single most important issue we face as a global community.'	What is the G8?
This is why climate change was a priority during the UK's G8 Presidency, along with Africa.	
The G8 leaders signed a statement, which included an agreement to 'act with resolve and urgency now.' This was the first time G8 leaders reached an agreement on the role of human activity in global warming and the need for urgent action.	
The statement also included an agreement that greenhouse gas emissions need to slow down and stop and that G8 countries need to make 'substantial cuts' in emissions.	Which of the machines that people use give out these 'emissions'?
The statement also included a package of measures to combat climate change. The package includes: – improvements to energy efficiency in appliances and buildings – cleaner vehicles – work on developing cleaner fuels, renewable energy and promoting research and development – and the financing of future projects.	
The UK Government says it intends to carry on trying to make these changes. The first meeting held in London aimed to transform how people use energy so we can have a secure and sustainable energy future.	Why does the government want to change the way that energy is used?

Time Lines

Roughly:

? million years ago, when dinosaurs held sway	Primate family appears. Our earliest ancestors skittered through the trees and bushes, much as squirrels do today
5-7 million years ago	Human – ape ancestors.
4 million years ago	Bipedal, human-like species
2 million years ago	Homo erectus appears – dramatic improvement in quality and range of tools – very simple hand axes
	Third order intentionality appears? (Dunbar p.75)
	Controlled use of fire?
	Two species of chimp separate
	Brain doubles in size
500,000 years ago	Homo Sapiens – larger brain, lighter body build
	Fourth order intentionality appears?
150,000 – 200,000 years ago	Anatomically modern humans
	Fifth order intentionality? (Dunbar p.76)
	Small group of about 5000 females (and about the same number of males) living in Africa, from whom all 5 billion of us modern humans have descended
80,000 years ago	Fossil evidence that early modern humans and Neanderthals had enlarged thoracic vertebral canal associated with development of speech.
50-40,000 years ago (about 100, 000 years after the human brain reaches its modern size)	Homo Sapiens (us) come into being. Upper Palaeolithic Revolution – sudden change – knifelike blades, borers, arrowheads
30,000 years ago	Statues, art appearing – earliest cave paintings
28,000 years ago	Neanderthals die out
25,000	Willendorf Venus
20,000 years ago	Awls, needles, Venus figurines
	Abri dwellings
18,000 years ago	Cave paintings – Lascaux
14,000 years ago	Cave painting – Font de Gaume
12,000 years ago	People stopped painting in caves – appearance of stone megaliths in southern Turkey decorated with wild animals best seen by firelight. Farming also seems to originate in this time and place – DNA of most widely used wheat today has its origins in that time and place (to feed the huge gatherings that would take place around the megaliths?)

Time Lines (continued)

After 3000 years of hunter gatherers, a major climate change. Nomadic peoples forced to move towards water. Egypt one of first civilisations – the regularity of the flooding of the Nile enabled them to settle and flourish around 5000 BC

4000 BC	6000 years ago	
3500 BC	5500 years ago	Wheel invented in Mesopotamia First use of plough – Hunter gatherers settle down By the end of the fourth millennium BC, Uruk had become the largest urban centre in Mesopotamia if not the world. The story of Gilgamesh is probably attached to a real king – Gilgamesh, fifth in line of the First Dynasty of kingship of Uruk following the great flood recorded in the epic, placing him approximately in the latter half of the third millennium. He was known as the builder of the wall of Uruk. According to the king list, his father was a high priest of Kullab, a district of Uruk, from whom he derived his mortality
2700 BC		
3100-2900		Sumerian Cuneiform appears in Mesopotamia (Philadelphia tablet)
2500 BC	4500	Grave not far from Stonehenge – gold ornaments – bones of a man from central Europe – Stonehenge built then?
2100 BC		The story of Gilgamesh was widely known in area of Mesopotamia – several Sumerian versions of the story
1894 BC	4000 years ago	Babylon developed into a city state in Mesopotamia. First ever system of writing (cuneiform), maths, pottery kilns, first to use metal. King Hammurabi gathered laws and wrote them down – the code of Hammurabi. Gilgamesh – the first ever story – written
1800-1600		Clay mask of Humbaba (Huwawa) Ancient Greek art – bodies like gods
700 BC		More life like figurines – fusing of Egyptian and Greek arts
668-627 BC		Ashurbanipal, King of Assyria Gilgamesh was recorded in a standardised Akkadian version in the seventh century BC, and stored in the famous library of King Ashurbanipal
0		
1844		Mounds of Nineveh discovered (Mesopotamia)
1850s	155 years ago	Crimean War
1853		First fragments of Gilgamesh discovered
1870		Franco Prussian War Barnados opens home for children
1871		Siege of Paris Dr Livingstone and Stanley meet in Africa Darwin Trades Union Act legalises Trades Unions in Britain Alice in Wonderland
1872		Artillery at Stonehenge in *Illustrated London News* Smith cracks the code of the ancient writing, in the British Museum, enabling him to read the earliest account of the story of Gilgamesh.

Garden Design Guide

How will the gardens of Uruk grow?

Will you arrange the plants systematically:

- according to what kind they are?
- according to how they will be used?
- to tell a 'story'? Who will be able to 'read' this story?

Does the garden contain any secrets?

Also:

- what will the garden be used for: pleasure, special occasions, growing things to eat or to show?
- who will be using it: ordinary people, the king?
- how will it suit the climate: will there be shade, what kind of soil?
- how will you keep it watered: by canals, underground systems, pipes...?
- where will you store such things as tools, seeds, cut flowers?

There are four important steps to garden design:

Start with a base map

A *base map* is a plan of the property showing :

- the location in the city
- its orientation to the sun
- other structures on the site

Incorporate shade into the design

Shade from trees keeps the landscape cooler, reduces water loss, and helps create a comfortable living environment. A shaded landscape may be 20oF cooler than a landscape in full sun.

Walking beneath a shade tree gives immediate relief from the sun as the tree acts like an umbrella. If the tree is growing in moist soil, it not only blocks heat but also dissipates heat by evaporative loss from the leaves. Structures like trellises, arbours, walls, and fences can also provide shade. Shading makes the landscape more water efficient.

Plan areas for different uses

Will there be public and private areas?

The *public* area is the area most visitors see, such as at the entrance.

The *private* area will be for the use of the gardeners and the king.

The *service* area is the working or utility area, usually screened from view and may contain items such as waste, compost, and equipment.

Choose plants that fit the design

Select plants to fill the garden. It is important to space plants far enough apart so they can achieve their mature size without being crowded. Remember to leave lanes for picking the fruit at harvest time.

Reflection and Response

In Expressive Arts GCSE this term we have been:

- responding to the stimulus, the story of *Gilgamesh*
- responding in three different art forms: drama, dance and music
- learning to use elements of the art forms: *atmosphere, narrative, symbol*
- exploring and developing ideas, planning work and communicating our ideas.

Atmosphere	Mood, feeling. The atmosphere will have an impact on the feelings of the audience, and maybe on the senses e.g. a piece of music that creates a feeling of tension, a dance that is joyous
Narrative	A story or having something to say; what you want to get over to the audience
Symbol	Something that represents something else, or reminds you of it. It can remind you of a feeling, a character, an object or an event. For example, the dove is the symbol of peace, a musical instrument can symbolise a character, gesture can symbolise power

Here are some of the ways you have practised using *atmosphere* in your lessons:

1. You have created the shadows of Gilgamesh and the gardener – the shadows that tell the truth – you were showing what it feels like to work in that garden and be with the king.

2. You have created the beginning of a song that expresses something of what life is like for the people in the story.

3. You have created the mood of the waterhole, and of the destruction of the cedar forest.

Here are some of the ways you have practised using *narrative* in your lessons:

1. You created depictions of what it is like for the people of Uruk as Gilgamesh moves through the city – you were showing what the story is communicating to us.

2. You have developed the context of the story through narrative dance, imagining how the people dance for Gilgamesh.

3. You have developed the characters in the story by imagining their life and work as you created the gardens.

Here are some of the ways you have practised using *symbol* in your lessons:

1. You have created a short scene showing the possibilities of what Enkidu could become – you used movement (sign) and cloth to symbolise the ideas of e.g. warrior or king

2. You have created in dance the quality of water moving as separate parts and as a whole.

3. You have experimented with representing the idea of the characters (e.g. Enkidu) with a musical instrument.

The Freedom Museum of Human Being
Attention: Students of Gilgamesh

Dear Pupils

It has come to our attention that you have recently been studying the story of Gilgamesh. We were very pleased to hear this. We have long regarded this story as one of the most important stories in the history of humankind. It is, as far as we know, the first story ever written, and contains important clues about the human race.

Our centre has recently received some money as part of a government plan. This plan will support people in the Broader Middle East and North Africa. It will go to help 20 million more people become literate by 2015.

Our part in this plan is to run a scheme to encourage people to take an interest in reading. We also want to encourage them to read about the history of the people.

We will soon be having the first meeting to plan our scheme. Our meeting will be in Bahrain in November 2005, and we wanted to invite a UK group of young people to make a short presentation.

We would like to commission *you* to make the short presentation. We would like your presentation to show what you have found out so far about the human race, and why exploring the story of Gilgamesh has helped you make connections.

With your permission, I would like to hold a meeting with you to discuss this.

Yours in hope
K. Hammurabi
Director

Some beliefs about the Cedar

In addition to its significant role in the Epic of Gilgamesh, the Cedar of Lebanon is regarded as a world tree in several mythological passages. The cutting of the cedar is seen as the destruction of world-empires – really, as the end of history. The pitch of the cedar was utilised for easing the pain of toothaches. The sawdust of the cedar puts snakes to flight, and thus makes sleeping under the shade of a cedar a relatively safe siesta. Some think the cedar was used in the preservation of corpses in ancient Egypt.

The Cedar of Lebanon aided society not only culturally but as the basis of numerous economies for ancient civilisations. It was used for the construction of temples, palaces and boats. The export of cedar wood to Egypt was an important factor in the growth of Phoenician prosperity and provided capital to launch ambitious enterprises in international trading, navigation, and arts and crafts.

The essential oil is believed to have antiseptic properties, mainly for the respiratory system.

Section Four

Possibilities in Such Times
The Teacher and TIE
Notes on a Connective Curriculum

Possibilities in Such Times

In 2002 the governments of the USA and the UK ignored public opinion and began a war against Iraq. In the UK the build up to the war had resulted in unprecedented mobilisation of young people's opinions into collective, public action. On the day war was declared, young people, up and down the country affirmed their opposition to it by leaving their schools and joining with others to make public demonstrations of their thoughts and feelings.

The variety of response by adult authority to this concern shown by our young people was telling:

- One school in Leicester had police at the gates to prevent the young people from leaving the premises

- Other schools viewed participation in this significant world event as truanting and penalised students who took part

- Our own school, following an NUT meeting which voted to support the action, allowed not just the students to join the local demonstrations but made it possible for staff to accompany them, with other staff covering them.

What was each of these schools teaching their students that day?

As noted in the introduction to *Stating the Obvious*, schools have a responsibility to enable children to learn about war. Our society has been living in a state of war throughout the time I have been teaching. History tells me that this has been the case for a very long time. It also tells me that as each decade passes, war is increasingly capable of widespread devastation.

The adolescent brain is at a crucial stage of development. It is putting down the hard wiring, and abilities and ways of being human are becoming fixed. We must grasp every possible opportunity to fashion a curriculum that will help young people to live, not simply survive, in the 21st century.

I produced the following material for teachers in our school when the USA attacked Afghanistan in 2001. The management of the school distributed the material to all staff.

There are times when world events suddenly reveal an alarming, and at times terrifying, prospect for our pupils. They can appear controversial too. It is not unusual for teachers to feel unable and unqualified to address such issues. Neither is it unusual for teachers to want or need to stay on target with the planned curriculum. This is understandable, for many reasons. But if teachers do not address such issues, who will?

So how can teachers approach these apparently overwhelming issues? How can they meet the needs of their pupils in such times?

The following pages offer some questions that subject teachers could raise in order to focus teacher thinking and pupil learning in difficult times. They are based upon a 'snapshot' of the curriculum in our school at the start of the war on Afghanistan. The questions are offered as a model or an approach. Their aim is to keep the needs and experience of the child at the centre.

NB: What the pupils actually do will depend on the nature of the subject/skill:

e.g. design, write, discuss, model, think etc

History

Year 7

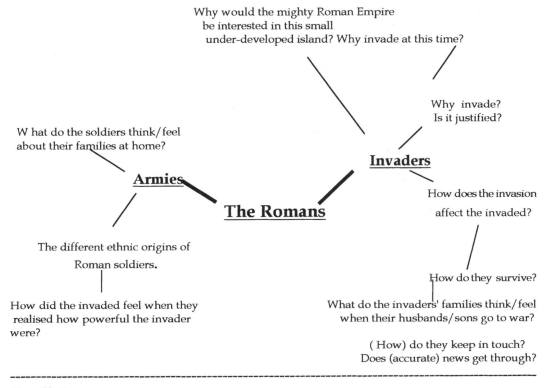

Why would the mighty Roman Empire
be interested in this small
under-developed island? Why invade at this time?

Why invade?
Is it justified?

W hat do the soldiers think/feel
about their families at home?

Invaders

Armies

How does the invasion

affect the invaded?

The Romans

The different ethnic origins of
Roman soldiers.

How do they survive?

How did the invaded feel when they
realised how powerful the invader
were?

What do the invaders' families think/feel
when their husbands/sons go to war?

(How) do they keep in touch?
Does (accurate) news get through?

English

Year 7

Who else in the world could use Skellig's help?

What strengths doe s Michael have?

Saviours

Skellig
(A novel)

Are there other ways that people
in trouble can be helped?

Survivors

What strategies does the family have
for surviving its troubles?

Who else could have
helped this family?
What did the neighbours think of them?

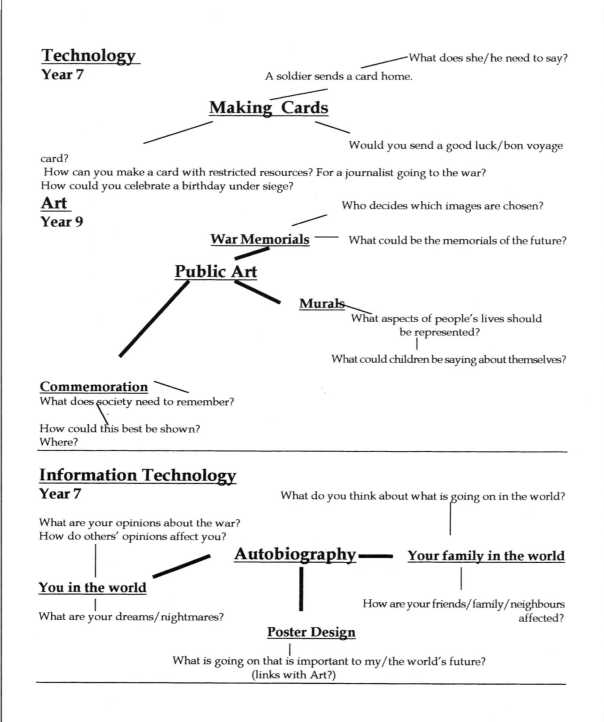

Technology
Year 7

A soldier sends a card home. ———What does she/he need to say?

Making Cards

Would you send a good luck/bon voyage card?

 How can you make a card with restricted resources? For a journalist going to the war?
How could you celebrate a birthday under siege?

Art
Year 9

Who decides which images are chosen?

War Memorials —— What could be the memorials of the future?

Public Art

Murals

What aspects of people's lives should be represented?

What could children be saying about themselves?

Commemoration
What does society need to remember?

How could this best be shown?
Where?

Information Technology
Year 7

What do you think about what is going on in the world?

What are your opinions about the war?
How do others' opinions affect you?

Autobiography —— **Your family in the world**

You in the world

What are your dreams/nightmares?

How are your friends/family/neighbours affected?

Poster Design

What is going on that is important to my/the world's future?
(links with Art?)

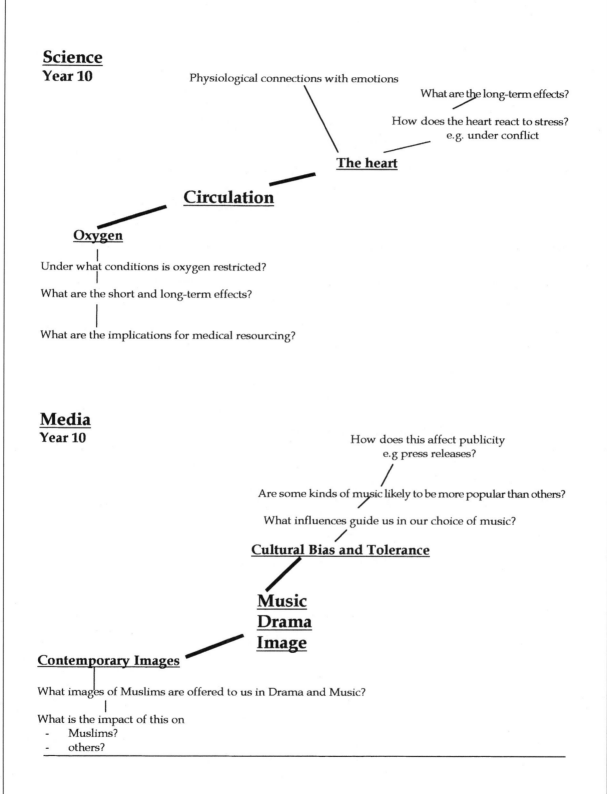

Science
Year 10

Physiological connections with emotions

What are the long-term effects?

How does the heart react to stress?
e.g. under conflict

The heart

Circulation

Oxygen

Under what conditions is oxygen restricted?

What are the short and long-term effects?

What are the implications for medical resourcing?

Media
Year 10

How does this affect publicity
e.g press releases?

Are some kinds of music likely to be more popular than others?

What influences guide us in our choice of music?

Cultural Bias and Tolerance

Music
Drama
Image

Contemporary Images

What images of Muslims are offered to us in Drama and Music?

What is the impact of this on
- Muslims?
- others?

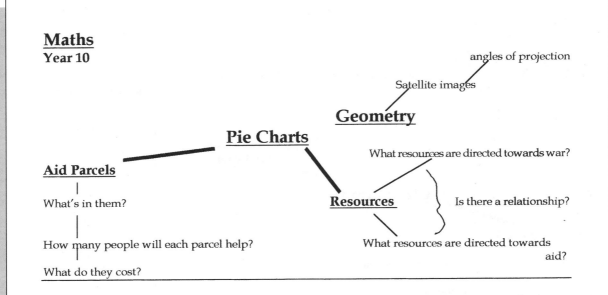

Maths
Year 10

angles of projection

Satellite images

Geometry

Pie Charts

What resources are directed towards war?

Aid Parcels

Resources

Is there a relationship?

What's in them?

How many people will each parcel help?

What resources are directed towards aid?

What do they cost?

Drama

Year 9	**Sula and Nel**	*The Journal for Drama in Education* Vol 17 Issue 2	Page and Elston
Year 10	**Here's Much to do with Hate, But More with Love**	*The Journal for Drama in Education* Vol 18 Issue 1	Grady
Year 12	**Our Country's Good**	*The Journal for Drama in Education* Vol 18 Issue 1	Williams

The Teacher and TIE

In November 2005, Theatre in Education (TIE) celebrated its 40th anniversary in the UK with a conference entitled *Rare Earth – Rich Explorations*, at Warwick Arts Centre. During the conference one of the participants said:

> *I have been thinking back over my Theatre in Education experiences in school. I was pleased to realise that I'd actually had quite a few, from sitting in a grassy field at age 6 listening to a storyteller with his live horse, to sitting in a school hall aged 13 watching a play set in WWII. But the most memorable, engaging, satisfying, and self-questioning was a program of work done by a company called Theatr Fforwm Cymru. They visited many times over a 6-week period, presenting performance elements, and facilitating workshops, discussions and debates. This concluded with a handover of responsibility to us to do the work with younger years in the school. I think it was memorable for me because we were being asked to take action, we were being asked to take responsibility and our opinions were honestly being asked for – something that I wasn't used to. So what in my opinion are the main aims in creating Theatre in Education? Assisting young people to make sense of the world around them through taking action. Assisting them in not what to think, but how to think – both for themselves and socially.*

Theatre in Education shares the same common ancestry that Drama has with education. At the highest point of its development, its richness and potency go straight to the heart of what it is to be human. In TIE one teacher alone does not manage the creative social process for a class of students. A company of actor/teachers, a director, a set designer and a writer manages it. It is a highly developed pedagogy, as I hope to illustrate with the following account of *The King, the Crow, and the Girl* by Theatr Powys.

Theatr Powys is a TIE Company in Powys, in Wales. In 2005 they toured a programme called *The King, the Crow and the Girl* to primary school children. As with most of their programmes, there were two versions of the play, one in Welsh and one in English, each with its own acting company. In October 2005 they took the programme further abroad, incorporating another language.

The King, the Crow and the Girl
by Theatr Powys

An observer's account of one day's programme, with notes for teachers.

The notes for teachers highlight something of the art and craft of the director and actor/teachers in the Theatre in Education Company. They also, it is hoped, demonstrate methodological possibilities for the lone practitioner.

The italicised quotes are representative, verbatim (translated) examples of what was said on the day.

Outside in the school playground, a teacher talks with his class. The children are about 10 years old.

Photograph 2 shows members of the company and a local teacher preparing the nest

The desks and chairs are gone from the children's classroom.

In their place is a huge circle of straw, twigs and leaves. In one place on the circle there is a small bird's nest, placed next to a branch covering a log. Inside the nest is a dull, metal crown encircling five 'crow' eggs.

Black feathers stick up out of the nest circle. They are 'crow' feathers.

The stage is set and it is big enough to hold everyone.

Photograph 1 gives a crow's view of the children outside in the playground.

They have come to their school for a special occasion, on a particular day. The day is particular because the teachers are on strike and so the school is closed. They are the only children in school. The occasion is special because a TIE Company has come to work with them. It is called Theatre Powys, and has come from Wales. The children live in the city of Gjilan, in Kosova. They speak Albanian.

Inside, the actor/teachers are preparing a nest.

As with educational drama, there is a circle in which the potential of all is signified and the significance of all is symbolised.

This differs importantly from the physical layout of most theatre performances. For the most part these events are organised so that the majority of the participants are turned with their faces in one direction, with one focal point for all activity, all attention. In the circle, however, we can each see and be seen by each one of the others. This tells the class that they are not audience – they are participants.

Photograph 3 shows the large nest circle

Alongside the Company are others: teachers from Gjilan who have already taken part in the programme and are eager to support it as it travels to other schools. There is also an observer – a teacher from England.

The class teacher brings the children into a classroom with desks and chairs, where they wait. The Company have planned how they will enter the classroom and how they will stand – careful attention is paid to the effect all these adults might have on the children. As they enter the classroom they are careful to greet the children, not overwhelm them. The adults introduce themselves. Some have learnt to greet in Albanian. Some are helped by an interpreter.

> The attitude of the Company towards the children is one of respect for them, in both their individual and their collective being.
>
> There is a high degree and order of preparation. There is a skilled use of theatre sign ready and in place, and there is shared reflexivity, born of shared experience and guided by the director. This rests on a pedagogical stance that places the needs of the children at the centre of each segment of activity. This first encounter is crucial in the building of creative trust.

One of the actor teachers is about to begin the story. He plays the role of the storyteller. He is from Gjilan and has worked in Wales with Theatre Powys. This programme will be done mostly in Albanian, with a little English, so much rests on him.

The storyteller begins to speak about the story – the class are immediately wrapt. The observer can see that every single one of the children, and their teacher, is engaged.

The storyteller invites the class to follow him out of the classroom and along the corridor to the classroom where the nest circle is waiting. As they enter the room with the nest circle, the children's faces register a mixture of delight, caution and admiration. Sitting in the nest circle, next to the bird's nest is an actor/teacher 'bird', a crow. Her signing is gentle, low key, and approachable. There is a sound track – a rich mix of bird, music and something not quite identifiable.

The storyteller invites the children to stand around the outside edge of the nest circle and the class are invited to tell what they can hear. The storyteller and the children speak quietly – they are being careful of the bird, and of the nest circle and they are edging in to the drama. Except for one girl, Miranda – she speaks in loud and ringing tones. She cuts through the hush. She says that the bird 'wants to be free'. She is very clear.

Her comments are, of course, treated with respect. The storyteller steps into the nest circle – he demonstrates a further edging in – one leg at a time. He picks up the bird's nest and shows it around the circle; in it are the eggs and the crown. The children are invited to step into the nest circle – they all do, some more cautiously than others – some step one leg at a time.

Again the class are invited to tell what they can see, this time in the bird's nest.

> The children are being led into the fiction by degrees. Their knowledge of birds, eggs, and the world is acknowledged and validated by the storyteller. Their expertise is shared. By this point the storyteller is working at many levels. He is preparing the ground for a story. He is using sign and symbol – material objects and imagined events. He is enabling the class of children to participate. He is working in Albanian and English so that the actor/teachers, and the observer, who don't speak Albanian, can understand the progress of the work.

The children are invited to make themselves comfortable, and there is music. The storyteller, seated on the log, opens the storybook. But he does not just open it. He opens it in stages, looking at the class, looking at the book. As he tells the story he tells of a girl in a city hurt by war. He tells of this girl who collects things in her bucket – broken things that carry echoes of the lives of the people of the city. He tells of a king and a blinding crown. The story is powerful and the children and their teacher are listening, hard.

There is an interruption. One or two heads turn and quickly return. All are *in* the story.

The interruption is caused by a boy who is late. The teacher goes to him, hugs him welcome, and seats him with the class. There is no questioning or criticism.

This boy is late because his home is on the other side of the border. It is not always easy to be on time for school when your home is across the border.

During the telling of the story the crow, still sitting by the bird's nest, signs moments of disturbance. At times she gives a silent caw. You could say it was like the silent scream.

The storyteller finishes the story and closes the book – again staged. He invites the children to step outside the nest circle. As they leave, many are more careful of the nest circle than when they entered – this time most of the children step carefully, one step at a time.

> The difference between the way in which the children enter and the way in which they leave the nest circle is telling.
> It tells that they are now in the fiction.
> It tells that they hold the nest in some regard.
> It tells that they feel safe and in control enough to be in control of themselves.
> The story, the telling of the story, the objects, the setting, and the actor/teachers' method have all worked to engage the children.

There is a break.

At the end of the break the storyteller fetches the children in from the playground and accompanies them back into the classroom. As they enter they can see two actor/teachers in the circle. They are talking and signing about the story; they are wondering and questioning. The storyteller moves into the nest circle to join them and the children are drawn into the wondering and questioning. They talk of where crows can be in a city, and they talk of what the crows in this story can see of this city.

> The two actor/teachers are wondering and questioning as 'story listeners'. What they are doing is re-locating the children in the story, enabling resonance between the world of the story and the material world, modelling that there are questions to be asked and validating the not-yet-knowing position that the children are in.

The children say what it is that the crows can see as they watch over this city. They say they can see:

> *'Cold children'*
> *'People bleeding'*
> *'Hungry children'*
> *'The names of the people who have died'.*

The children are making the story their own. The storyteller asks the children:

'How does a crow watch – how does a crow listen?'

As the children give their answers the teacher/actors are moving into 'crow'. The children begin to stand and become crow.

The storyteller says

'All through the war the crows watched.'

The actor/teachers sign 'crow watching'.

'All through the war the crows listened.'

The actor/teachers sign 'crow listening'.

'After the war the crows watched.
After the war the crows listened.'

The actor/teachers continue signing 'crow'

'The crows took to the air.'

There is music and the actor/teachers sign and invite the crow children to take to the air.

The storyteller narrates the crows into settling on the nest circle, each taking up a position by a crow feather.

The storyteller welcomes them to the crow conference. He is conducting the conference. He is crow.

> This form of engagement was clearly a new experience for the children. They enjoyed moving around the circle in unison with the actor/teachers, as though they were flying. Some were self-conscious, yet smiled, some used dance patterns to move themselves along, and others were totally engrossed in the flying.

At the conference the crows are invited to make reports. To show that they would like to speak they must hold the crow feather out, a touchstone for participation.

The boy who was late says that he, as crow, has seen

'Bones in the lakes'.

The actor/teachers model and build upon the children's contributions – the momentum builds and they split off into groups so that all can speak and be heard. These are called wing groups.

As the crow conference reconvenes and the crows report back from their wing groups, the speaking gathers import – the crow children are invited to step into the circle as they make their points. They say:

'The trees are cut'
'The children run out of the city'
'The mothers cry'
'I can see a little girl collecting'
'She wants to remember what has happened'.

One girl crow straddles the nest circle. She has not yet been called upon to speak but she can hardly wait. Many of the children who come into the circle to speak stand with their weight on one leg and one arm slightly behind them. They are halfway in character, but fully determined to make their point.

An actor/teacher says:

'The crows are like people – how can they live like this?'

The crow children's comments come thick and fast:

'There are bodies in the river'
'We crows need to help the people'
'Mothers go secretly to send food to the soldiers in the mountains'
'I saw the little girl helping the crows'
'They are burying people alive'

The observer bends low over her notebook. For a moment she cannot write. She cannot look up. She does not want to let the children see that the weight of what they know about the world is overwhelming her.

When she at last looks up, things are moving on. One of the actor/teachers has moved to one side and is ready as the girl.

The crows are discussing what to do with the king's crown and how to bring the girl to the conference. They decide to hide the crown in the nest circle, and they plan what to say to her to make her feel safe.

A delegation of crows 'flies' off to bring her to the crow conference. Although only three are sent, many of the other crow children sign flying too. They are *in* the story.

As the girl arrives, the crow children reassure her:

'You are safe with us'
'Don't be afraid – this is like your home'
'We want to save you'
'We are not as bad as people think we are'
'Whatever you want we will get for you'
'You are like our parent'
'You help us and we will help you'.

The girl settles into the nest circle and the atmosphere is reassuring.

It is time for the lunch break.

> The children's comments from their standpoint as crows demonstrate the levels of engagement. The role of crow has given them a very particular viewpoint. It is both distant, and therefore protective, and yet all-seeing and gimlet sharp. If the children wish it, there is nothing that a crow can't witness. The sharpness of their vision allows for detail. As is evident from what the children say, there are a number of stances and investments. There is no one point of view.

Photograph 4 shows the girl with the objects.

As they leave the classroom the children pause in the doorway to look back – a threshold moment of reflection: '*what are the objects saying to the girl?*'

After lunch the children rush in. They are excited. One boy tells the storyteller that during the lunch hour he had dreamt of the crows – that he was a crow, flying.

The crow conference reconvenes. The feathers are held aloft – crow children begin to speak of what it is that the objects say to the girl. Two of the objects are a small, red, twisted, plastic spoon and the stump of a used candle. They say such things as:

'*The King tortures his people to become rich.*'
'*Thank you – you who saved us*'
'*The king has spoons, the people do not*'

An actor/teacher crow says

'*The spoon tells the story of the men who sit in the café. They have forgotten what it is to be free – I don't know – what does freedom mean?*'

The crow children continue:

'*The people don't need that any more – they used to take money and spend it on glasses of drink*'

An actor/teacher crow says

'*Do they not need money to be free?*'

The children continue

'*The king doesn't care for the people*'
'*The candle used to make light for when the power went off*'.

As each crow child speaks, they step into the circle. It is plain that the children are secure in their crow role. They no longer stand with their weight on one leg and one arm slightly behind them. They stand securely on two feet, arms gesturing with the power of their words. Increasingly the children speak the words in heightened story mode. They are not just *in* the story – they are making it, they are driving it.

When the Company chose the objects, they chose them carefully. Members of the company knew that in Gjilan there are many men who spend their days sitting in a café, stirring one coffee after another with plastic spoons. The coffees have to last a long time. Spoons get twisted when hands lie idle. They knew also that in Gjilan the power is cut, without warning, at any time of the day and night, and just about every day and night.

In the same way the members of the Company are selecting concepts to place in front of the children.

The conference gathers momentum. It is decided that the crows will bring the King to the conference. There is the question of where the eggs and the crown should be placed. On this occasion the crown is hidden under the straw.

The storyteller crow flies to fetch the King and bring him to the nest circle. This is dangerous. The King resists. It is a struggle for the storyteller crow but he brings back the King and deposits him in the centre of the nest circle.

There is a pause.

The King lunges at the girl, whipping her feet out from under her and grabbing at the crown she is clinging to. Despite the pain she is in, she does not make a sound – like so many children.

The crow children begin to tell the king

'*People are suffering because of you*'

'*You are not the king that you should be – we need another king to give the people freedom*'

'*You need to listen to the people – if you won't behave, we won't behave*'

An actor/teacher holds up one of the objects from the bucket and says:

'This object will tell you history'.

The King says

'Forget history – draw a line – move forward not back'.

The crow children, holding objects from the bucket up to him, tell the King:

'This tells you how the war is bad, because of you'

'This means there have been so many restaurants destroyed'

'This tells you our life, our future, and you are the one who is stopping that'

'We need the light'

'We're never going to forget the history'

'This tells you the people are destroyed'

'Freedom cannot be bought – it is the most expensive thing"

'This tells you the blood of the people – all the people are bleeding'

'You need to listen'

If you're not listening you're not even a human being'

'If you are not listening we will keep speaking'

'You can't stop us speaking'

'You need to share your money with the people'

'If you don't learn now you will learn later'

> As the actor/teachers demonstrate *how* the objects signify, so the children are able to locate key concepts through them. The statements of the crow children weave around each other, forming a poetic texture and stitching concrete images (blood of the people, destroyed restaurants) to concepts (war, freedom, history). They advance through accusation toward demand and determination – they are acutely aware of what they need in order to survive.

The King does not listen to what the crows are saying. He chooses his moment and lunges at the bird's nest, taking the eggs. He lunges at the girl, hurting her and taking the crown. He is loud, wild and violent. The girl places herself between the King and the crow children.

The storyteller breaks the moment: the children are invited back into the circle and the story from the book is concluded. Safe again and held in the nest circle.

There is a break.

When they return the children can see the King lying asleep in the centre of the nest circle. He has the crown on his head, he is cradling the nest and the eggs are on the floor, under his hand.

The children begin to speak.

Their words come bouncing out, one after another; they speak individually and chorally.

They are not in character. They are speaking as themselves.

An actor/teacher asks

'The king is angry with the crows – why?'

The children speak

'The crows disturbed him – speaking about their freedom – the people's freedom'

'He's not even keeping the eggs warm so they can hatch'

'He's worried – he doesn't want there to be more crows'

> Here the children are straddling the metaphor just as they have straddled the nest circle. They are both in the story and in the real world.

The children are invited to place the king differently – to manipulate the actor/teacher into another position, and to put the objects from the story in relation to him. Working together, the class give the King qualities like no other King.

'The book is a good history'. They place it, open, so that the king can see its contents.

'The King should smile'

'He should touch the eggs like the crows do'

An actor/teacher says

'See how close the history (the book) is to the future (the eggs) now'

> As these 10-year-old children are re-modelling the being of the King, they are learning how to manipulate a complex system of semiotics.

They conclude by saying what they can see now. Each sentence begins with:

'I can see a King who ...'

'Gave freedom to the birds'
'Makes sure the children are not hungry'
'Is wise and protects the eggs'
'Loves the wisdom and the happiness'
'Can be in the family of crows'
'Doesn't forget history'
'Keeps the eggs warm'.

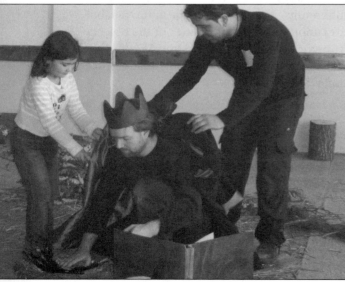

As the Company and the children bid farewell to each other, the children's class teacher says that this is a '*very developed pedagogy*'.

As the quote at the beginning of this section makes clear, this pedagogy is a memorable one. The conference participant who remembered the sheer thrill of being asked not only to give voice to her opinion but also to take responsibility and action, is now an actor/teacher with Theatr Powys. This chapter concludes with her words:

> *We had an exceptional experience in Kosovo last month with* The King The Crow and The Girl. *I saw the potential of Theatre in Education. It concretised for me why I do what I do and why I love what I do. I saw the potential of a TIE programme to give the young people the chance to express deep felt social and political discomfort with their situation. It gave them the opportunity to give voice to their passion, desire for justice, desire for freedom, human rights, their needs, feelings and frustrations in a hugely in-depth way. They were grappling with the question of 'what is freedom?' In the words of one of the Albanian children, when speaking about the 'leggy ones': 'they want their freedom, they just want their freedom...it is the most expensive thing'. It gave them the ability to ask the questions perhaps they didn't even know they wanted to ask. And if there was an answer to give they often gave the answer themselves. I saw the potential TIE has in assisting in the articulation of such things.*

> Naomi Doyle

Photographs 5 and 6 show the children placing the objects and the king in relation to each other.

Notes on a Connective Curriculum

To orientate toward understanding ourselves, the key experiences of being human must become central to the curriculum.
Notes on a Curriculum for Living by Geoff Gillham

The matter of the mind of the people, the matter of the being of the people, and the matter of the doing of the people
Dorothy Heathcote 1985

The past 25 years have seen numerous changes in schools in this country, each more product orientated and assessment centred than the last. For schools and teachers, these changes began in 1989 with the government imposed National Curriculum – the result of the 1988 Education Reform Act (ERA). Hot on the heels of ERA came the league tables – a system of comparing one school with another. Although schools and teachers experienced this narrative in this sequence, it seems that the sequence of intention was the reverse. The ideological purpose of the then government was to create competition between schools. And to do this a National Curriculum was necessary.

Confronted by this ideological bag of tricks, teachers have struggled, and still struggle, to make sense of an almost bewildering succession of upheavals that have, it seems, done their best to come between the children and us. To resist bewilderment and foster that which is human in our schools, we have to keep our eyes open.

As Stenhouse says: 'Teachers must be the critics of work in the curriculum, not docile agents' (Stenhouse, 1975 p.75).

We need to see the dangers posed by those who are settling for less and embracing the narrow, alienating remit of the National Curriculum. We have to take issue with what seems to be an increasingly desperate bid for assessment to nth degree. We cannot help but feel the gap left by those who despaired and left the profession. We should acknowledge that new young teachers are often ill prepared, thanks to reduced teacher education and lack of theoretical perspective.

At the same time, we should know that, since its inception, there has been resistance to the National Curriculum and its consequences and intentions. This story of resistance is a *lehrstucke* (learning play) (Brecht, 1930) in its own right, and should be written – it would take too long to tell here. Suffice it to say that many different pedagogues and practitioners have spoken out against the National Curriculum, and in defence of the young. In this new century schools and teachers are turning away from the National Curriculum and choosing their own. As headteacher Patrick Hazelwood puts it:

> who would sensibly sanction a curriculum that resembles a long dark tunnel, running parallel to numerous other dark tunnels (none of which ever meet) and expect the occupants to relish the challenge of getting to the other end? (Hazelwood 2005)

Hazelwood, and the teachers with whom he works, have recreated that which seemed to have been lost, the 'freedom to educate in a way that places the needs of the learner at the forefront of our thinking' (*ibid*).

In fact, drama departments in secondary schools have long had the opportunity to shape their own curriculum. At Key Stage 3, the National Curriculum suggests a series of acquirable skills for Drama, but it does not offer prescribed programmes of study that address content, concepts or particular texts. At Key Stage 4, departments can choose which GCSE courses to follow, and thus choose texts and content. Some GCSE courses actively advocate a learner-centred approach to teaching even though they are an examination syllabus.

What then does the school drama department use as a guideline for structuring the drama curriculum?

I would like to offer the following for discussion.

Resisting Bewilderment

Confronted by the disconnecting effects of the ideological constraints in school, and the economic and political challenges lived through by the children, I have found the creation of a drama curriculum that is connective to be a necessity. As ideological descendants of Bruner, child-centred practitioners should seek to secure the reverse of the parallel tunnels deplored by Hazelwood. They should create continuity from one school-learning year to the next, i.e. a spiral curriculum within a single department, with

the schemes of work creating a ripple effect and providing a widening and reflective understanding for our children as we teach them over successive years. Rather than 'delivering' a succession of separate events the curriculum should give shape to a process wherein key themes and concepts are visited and re-visited. Like the DNA of the developing child, the curriculum must bond together all that has gone before with all that is possible.

The DNA molecule has a structure like that of a double helix – two spiralling, entwining strands connected by a series of ladder-like rungs running up the centre. Each spiral strand comprises a sugar phosphate backbone and an attached base, the latter forming half of each rung. The link between each of the bases is a hydrogen bond.

We can use the double helix of the DNA molecule as a model to illustrate how the hydrogen of the curriculum bonds the strand of the world to the strand of the child.

If we take this view of the curriculum (see below), seeing it as a way of enabling young people to know and live in their world, we have to establish common and fundamental curriculum components. I have found those identified by Geoff Gillham in his *Notes on A Curriculum for Living* a useful framework (see Table 1).

Strand 1	Hydrogen bonds	Strand 2
Existence	**The curriculum**	**The developing child**
The key experiences of being human – the three matters referred to by Heathcote (*ibid*). The material world.	The choice of what to learn and how to teach it. Where do we place the needs of the learners?	In the constant conference where the discourse between the imagination and experience/ consciousness takes place and where reason and understanding and future action are produced. This process takes place in the company of others, whether or not they are actually present.

Table 1: Fundamental Curriculum Components

A   Concepts: exploring and explaining, understanding and grasping

B   Skills:
1   Thinking
2   Accessing knowledge and communicating understanding
3   Physical and sensorimotor.

C   Learning Material: knowledge, subject matter

So how do we build these components into a curriculum? How do we structure the living interconnection of the world and the self – of play and image, where the taking of concrete sensory objects as pivots (e.g. doll as baby, or table as cave) and the manipulation of ideal forms (map as labyrinth, drawn kitchen objects as setting) as support for the development of the imagination and the formation of the new.

As Geoff Gillham (1995) says: 'A theory of Drama can only have viability, traction if it includes the actuality of the school/situation within in it'.

By looking again at the curriculum I have been teaching through schemes of work such as those outlined in this book, and by reading through some of the arts examination courses currently taught in schools at Key Stage 4 and

---

Table 2: Key Elements from public examination syllabi

	Concepts	Skills	Knowledge
KS5 *Performance Studies* 'A' and AS GCE OCR	**Essential elements** **Relationship** between the three art forms of dance, drama and music. **Interaction** of the art forms of dance, drama and music.	Practical knowledge of **elements.** **Ways** in which intentions are realised. **Methods** of creating performance work in a given style or genre. **Use** of **conventions** and methods. **Methods** of refining work into a coherent structure. Rehearsal **methods** and discipline. **Evaluation** of how theory works in practice.	**Knowledge** of essential elements. **Conventions** and methods of creating performance work Performance **repertoire** Performance **genres** Performance **theory**
Drama and Theatre Studies 'A' and AS GCE Edexcel	Drama and theatre texts have a **range** of **meanings.** How plays **relate to the contexts.** Ways in which plays are interpreted.	**Acting, designing, directing, interpreting.** **Creating, devising and improvising.** **Analytical, evaluative and critical** skills. **Communication.** **Inter-personal and group working.** **Use** of theatrical forms and genre.	**Plays and contexts** **Different way in which plays** are interpreted **Drama and theatre texts** **Theatrical forms and genre**

Table 2: Key Elements from public examination syllabi (continued)

	Concepts	Skills	Knowledge
KS4 *Drama* GCSE OCR	**Interpret and understand meaning and atmosphere.**	**Select and employ genres, styles.** **Ability to use elements.** **How** the language, signs and symbols of theatre are used to communicate dramatic meaning and atmosphere. **Reflect** and **analyse** their own and others' work, **taking action where appropriate to improve it.**	**Genres, styles and conventions** **Elements** of dramatic planning **Language, signs and symbols** of theatre **Range of scripts**
Expresssive Arts GCSE OCR	**Understanding of the interaction** between the art forms used.	**Produce a plan, consider alternatives and refine** ideas Exploration of **skills, processes and techniques.** **Select genre and style, and shape and structure ideas into a workable realisation.** **Communicate ideas** in appropriate art forms. **Reflect.**	**Culture and history** **Exploration and Development** **Art forms** **Atmosphere, Audience, Structure and Shape** **Narrative, Motif** **Genre, Symbol.**

Key Stage 5, I saw that one can begin to identify key curriculum elements.

By using the fundamental components in table 1 to organise the key elements from table 2, we can begin to categorise an approach.

Table 3: An approach to the curriculum.

Concepts	Skills	Knowledge
Essence.	Practical application of knowledge of elements.	Essential elements
Arts Forms.	Ways in which intentions are realised.	Conventions and methods of creating
Symbol.	Methods of planning, creating, devising, composing.	Repertoire – works of art
The interconnectedness of people/groups/ art forms.	Use and selection of conventions, form and genre and techniques.	Form, style, genre, conventions
The interconnectedness of art and social and political history.	Particular performance/expressive skills.	Contextualising information, cultural and historical.
The whole and the part.	Method of refining work into a coherent structure.	Different ways in which works have been interpreted.
Interpretation.	Deadlines.	Texts/set studies can have a range of meanings.
Ethos (atmosphere).	Evaluation of how theory works in practice.	Language, signs and symbols
Post Modernism.	Reflecting and analysing.	Elements of planning.
Modernism.	Evaluative and critical commentary.	World events.
What it is to be human.	Communicating meaning.	History.
	Inter-personal and group working.	Legend and myth.
	Presentation of creative/expressive work.	

Using this approach, it's not a huge leap to begin to fashion a snapshot of a curriculum that connects Key Stage 3 to Key Stages 4 and 5.

Table 4a: KS3 – Snapshot – Notes

Concepts	Skills	Knowledge
Form.	Explore and understand a range of ideas, issues, texts, and meanings.	Performance styles
Symbol (abstract).	Devising and improvising work as a member of a group.	Performance techniques and the appropriate technical vocabulary to discuss them
The interconnectedness of people/groups/ art forms.	Recognise potential in sources.	Some theoretical knowledge of essential elements of the performing arts
The whole and the part.	Methods of refining work into a coherent structure.	Ways in which intentions are realised in performance
Interpretation.	Working to informal performance deadlines in a lesson setting.	World events
Evolution.	Performance skills in each of the arts.	History
What it is to be human.	Performance techniques.	Legend and myth
Society.	Appraise and understand the purpose of the performing arts.	Society
Essence.	Ways in which intentions are realised in performance.	Works of art
Symbol.	Use of conventions and methods of creating performance.	
Atmosphere.	Communicate through the medium of the performing arts.	
Change.	Connections between the arts forms.	
Cause.		
War.		

From this simple snapshot we can begin to build in some detail that will connect the learning experience of the pupils.

Table 4b: KS3 – Some Detail of a Connective Drama Curriculum – Notes

Content and Concepts	Skills	Knowledge
Course 3 – Year 9? Evolution. Origins. What it is to be human. Truthfulness. Siege. Survival. Metamorphosis. Symbolic Acts. United Nations. Justice.	Discuss ideas. Express feelings. Listen effectively. Respond creatively to stimuli and develop the work. Create performance and improvise in a variety of groupings Role-play into character (showing dual attitudes). Gesture. Script/text realisation, interpretation of works. Use of style. Use of space between characters. Use of symbol Appropriate language, grammar, and inflexion. Evaluate use of form. Justify opinions. Consider wider implications and make connections within and beyond the work. Understanding of the way intention and meaning can be achieved through the use of techniques and skills, and that makes universal connections.	Scripts Legend and myth Historical Events World events Social phenomena Humans and nature and animals Creative method Contemporary culture
Course 2 – Year 8? What it is to be human. International relations. Ancestors/descendants. Oppression/freedom. Man's inhumanity to man. Human rights. Symbol. Dramatic tension. Spoken maps. Democracy. Responsibility. Nutrition.	Problem solving in large and small group. Responding thoughtfully to others. Responding to stimuli and developing the drama Creating and planning a group performance. Use of expressive movement, control (slow motion). Use of sound and silence. Establishing space (imaginatively) and place. Adopting and sustaining a role (showing attitudes). Conveying messages, giving instructions, connected narrative. Sequencing scenes and structuring action. Identifying sub-text. Asking and responding to questions. Commenting on what has been said. Seeing wider implications. Tensions. Applied vocabulary.	Legend and myth Historical events World events Social patterns Human behaviour Creative method Contemporary culture Slavery American history Black history The individual and society Food.

Table 4b: KS3 – Some Detail of a Connective Drama Curriculum – Notes (continued)

Content and Concepts	Skills	
Knowledge	Problem solving in a group.	Legend and myth.
Course 1 – Year 7	Engaging with creative work.	Social Interaction.
Content:	Developing story/plot.	Human behaviour.
Ownership of knowledge.	Working creatively with the class	Creative method.
Distributed intelligence.	as a whole. Listening and	Performance.
Application of technology.	responding creatively and socially	Material content of
Development of human being.	in small and large groups.	everyday objects.
Punishment/justice.	Developing creative work in a	
	small group. Rehearsing.	
Concepts:	Participating in a presentation.	
Knowledge.	Working through metaphor.	
Technological developments.	Taking on a mythic role.	
Human need.	Sustaining a role. Structuring	
Progress of human culture –	story – beginning, middle and	
change.	end. Working out matter.	
Story.	Reflecting on the work. Asking	
	questions.	
	Depiction into action.	
	Gesture of significant moments.	
	Movement to depict action.	
	Movement to express story.	

If, in the spirit of the spiral curriculum, we increase the complexity of application of the DNA model, we can apply it to the matter of the drama curriculum and add in the detail of the schemes of work (see Table 5 on pages 152-155).

In this way it is possible for a lone Drama department, indeed a lone Drama teacher, to develop their work and provide a cohesive whole for their students. As teachers continue to face the challenges laid down by successive, government-led reforms we need to be clear what we are teaching and why, for ourselves, and for the children.

Table 5: The Connective Drama Curriculum
Example schemes for Key Stages 3 and 4

Strand one: Content and concepts	Hydrogen bond: Imagination	Strand two: Artistry and skills		
What to learn	How and what to teach	How to learn		
Learning Material		Thinking – reason and understanding	Accessing knowledge and communicating understanding	Physical and sensory-motor
Content: Ownership of knowledge. Distributed Intelligence. Application of technology. Development of the human being. Punishment/justice.	**Prometheus SoW** Educational Drama Method. The myth of Prometheus. The material content of everyday objects. Technological change.	Developing story/plot. Working through metaphor. Structuring story – beginning, middle and end. Reflecting on the work. Asking questions. Applying metaphor. Working out matter.	Problem solving in a group. Working creatively with the class as a whole. Listening and responding creatively and socially in small and large groups. Creative work in a small group. Rehearsing. Participating in a presentation. Working through metaphor. Taking on a mythic role. Legend and myth. Material content of everyday objects.	Depiction into action. Gesture of significant moments. Movement to depict action. Movement to express story.
Concepts: Knowledge. Technology. Human need. Progress of Human Culture – change. Story.				

Table 5: The Connective Drama Curriculum (continued)
Example schemes for Key Stages 3 and 4

Strand one: Content and concepts	Hydrogen bond: Imagination	Strand two: Artistry and skills		
What to learn	How and what to teach	How to learn		
		Thinking – reason and understanding	Accessing knowledge and communicating understanding	Physical and sensory-motor
	Learning Material			
Content: Economic relationships. Family relationships – responsibility. Silenced expression. Cause and effect. Justice/revenge. Concepts: What it is to be human. Responsibility. Nutrition.	**The Cooks SoW** Educational Drama Method. The myth of Philomel. The unfolding of a family tragedy brought about by the consequences of war and the warrior stance, seen through the eyes of servants to the warrior.	Understanding cause and effect. Responding thoughtfully to others. Responding to stimuli and developing the drama. Identifying sub-text. Seeing wider implications. Use of symbol. Seeing wider implications.	Negotiating relationships. Problem solving in large and small groups. Responding to stimuli and developing the drama. Establishing space (imaginatively) and place. Adopting and sustaining a role (showing attitudes). Conveying messages, giving instructions, connected narrative. Sequencing scenes and structuring action. Identifying sub-text. Discussion Legend and myth. Food.	Responding to stimuli and developing the drama. Establishing space (imaginatively) and place. Physicalising a role (showing attitudes).

Table 5: The Connective Drama Curriculum (continued)

Example schemes for Key Stages 3 and 4

Strand one: Content and concepts	Hydrogen bond: Imagination	Strand two: Artistry and skills	
What to learn	How and what to teach	How to learn	
Learning Material	Thinking – reason and understanding	Accessing knowledge and communicating understanding	Physical and sensory-motor
Content: Differences and similarities between animals and humans. The relationship between humans and animals. Economic relationships. Justice/revenge. Consequences of war. Soldiers. **Concepts:** Evolution. War. Metamorphosis. What it is to be human. What is to be an animal.	**The Facility SoW** Educational Drama Method. The legend of Epimetheus. The legend of Lycaon. Animal being. Human being. The role of the soldier.	Research and reflection. Review, justify and analyse through discussion of differences and similarities. Begin to establish what might have happened to the past keeper. Through questioning the wolf, students will begin to consider connections; ask questions of Teacher-in-role. Synthesise elements of the drama through creating an ending.	Creation of characters through drafting and re-drafting. Work in double role. Synthesis of information imaginatively through description of smell. Complex manipulation of metaphor (sign and symbol). Legend. World events. Humans and animals.

Demonstration of character. Mimed use of an object, using sound and rhythm to enhance the drama.

Table 5: The Connective Drama Curriculum (continued)
Example schemes for Key Stages 3 and 4

Strand one: Content and concepts	Hydrogen bond: Imagination			Strand two: Artistry and skills
What to learn	How and what to teach	How to learn	Accessing knowledge and communicating understanding	Physical and sensory-motor
	Learning Material	Thinking – reason and understanding		
Content: The perception of self in relation to others. The actions of self in relation to others. How we understand our individual being and how we understand our social being. Human bonding. Justice. (Stewardship). Concepts: Human organisation. Innocence. Becoming Human. Change/ history. Cause.	**Gilgamesh SoW** Educational Drama Method The legend of Gilgamesh – the transformation of human society from hunter-gatherers to city dwellers, through the medium of the first recorded story. Expressive Arts forms.	*Generating ideas through exercising the creative imagination.* *Fostering curiosity, ingenuity and imagination in the shaping of ideas, experiences and feelings.* *Providing direct experience of the creative process.* *Working collaboratively in a group.*	*Stimulating, encouraging and sustaining candidates' confidence. Providing opportunities for active participation in the arts, paying particular attention to atmosphere, narrative and symbol. Working collaboratively in a group.*	*Stimulating, encouraging and sustaining candidates' confidence. Providing opportunities for active participation in the arts, paying particular attention to atmosphere, narrative and symbol. Working collaboratively in a group.*

Fostering that which is human in our schools

As well as striving to be clear about what we are doing in the drama department, we need also to be connecting with the rest of the school for at least two strong, inter-related reasons.

The first is the power of the learning medium. Both Vygotsky and Bruner have urged that the arts not be relegated to the position of icing on the cake but that they are, in themselves, central to the development of the brain. The arts are not *about* learning – they *are* learning. They are not subservient to other learning areas – they are whole *learnings* within themselves.

The second reason is 'mirror-neuron activity'. Recent research has revealed evidence of something Drama pedagogues have 'known' for a while: that there are a direct links between learning and observing, between speech and gesture. Experiments carried out during this research have catalogued observable brain cell activity. In the words of Anderson (2005):

> when we see someone carry out certain actions, the same parts of our brain are activated 'as if' we were doing it ourselves.

Conclusions are being drawn from this research that link the acquisition of speech and the ability to understand another, with the firing of mirror neurons by the observed gestures and behaviour of others. This is encouraging for drama teachers as it is implies a pedagogical development we should be grasping. It suggests a teaching methodology that understands the use of gesture and observed and observable behaviour.

These two reasons make it almost the duty of the drama teacher to reach out across traditional curriculum boundaries to others in school.

This chapter concludes with an example and a question. The example is of some of the concepts, learning materials and skills that Drama has in common with another subject, in this case Mathematics. The question is: how can educational drama method become both a stronger bond for the child's whole school experience, and a clearer voice in that continuous conference between experience and the imagination?

Drama and Maths – Shared Concepts in Learning

This concept map was sketched out during a school INSET session on Maths in the curriculum. It is only a beginning. At the heart and the brains of classroom drama lie the struggle to express, understand, explain and create relationships, between people and between people and the material world.

The same has been said of maths.

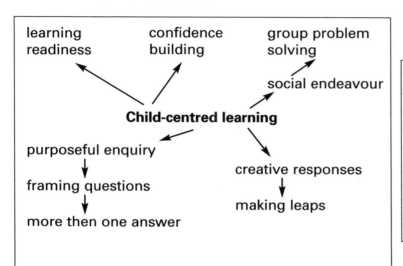

learning readiness   confidence building   group problem solving

social endeavour

Child-centred learning

purposeful enquiry

framing questions

more then one answer

creative responses

making leaps

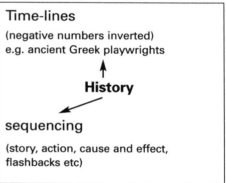

Time-lines
(negative numbers inverted)
e.g. ancient Greek playwrights

History

sequencing
(story, action, cause and effect, flashbacks etc)

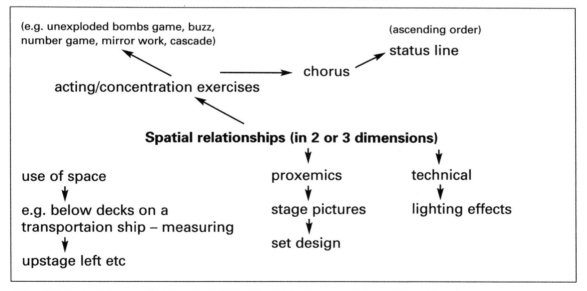

(e.g. unexploded bombs game, buzz, number game, mirror work, cascade)   (ascending order)
status line

chorus

acting/concentration exercises

Spatial relationships (in 2 or 3 dimensions)

use of space

e.g. below decks on a transportaion ship – measuring

upstage left etc

proxemics

stage pictures

set design

technical

lighting effects

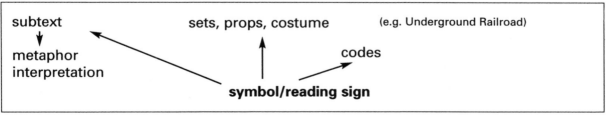

subtext   sets, props, costume   (e.g. Underground Railroad)

metaphor interpretation   codes

symbol/reading sign

References

Books and Journals

Airs, John and Ball, Chris (1998) A Cross Curricular Drama in O'Sullivan C. and Williams G. (eds), *Building Bridges* National Association for the Teaching of Drama

Anderson, Alun (2005) Behind The Mind's Mirror *The Economist* 1987-2006, 20th Edition

Bond, Edward (1965) *Saved* Methuen

Bond, Edward and Heathcote, Dorothy (1989) The Fight for Drama – The Fight for Education *Keynote Speeches from the NATD Conference 1989* National Association for the Teaching of Drama

Bond, Edward (2002) *The Cap Working Notes on Drama, the Self and Society* written for the National Conference of the National Association for the Teaching of Drama 2002

Bond, Edward (2004) Modern Drama and the Invisible Object *Journal for Drama in Education* vol. 20, issue 2

Bond, Edward (2005) On Censorship – The Iron Bolt in the Jaws *The Journal for Drama in Education* vol. 21, issue 2

Brecht, Bertolt trans. and ed. by J. Willet (1964) *Brecht on Theatre* Hill and Wang

Brecht, Bertolt (1930) *Measures Taken and Lehrstucke* Methuen (1977)

Bruner, Jerome (1986) *Actual Minds, Possible Worlds* Harvard University Press

Bruner, J. (1991) The Narrative Construction of Reality *Critical Inquiry* 18(1)

Bruner, J (1996) *The Culture of Education* Harvard University Press

Daniels, H. (ed) (1996) *An Introduction to Vygotsky* Routledge

Davis, David (ed) (2005) *Edward Bond and the Dramatic Child: Edward Bond's plays for young people* Trentham Books

Dawkins, Richard (1995) *River out of Eden* Wiedenfeld and Nicholson

Robin Dunbar (2004) *The Human Story* Faber and Faber

Eddershaw, Margaret (1996) *Performing Brecht* Routledge

Edexcel General Certificate of Education *Drama and Theatre Studies* Advanced Level

Euripides Morwood and Hall (eds) (2001) *The Trojan Women* Oxford World's Classics

Gillham, Geoff (1995) Notes on a Curriculum for Living *SCYPT Journal* no.30 June 1995 The Standing Conference for Young People's Theatre

Grady, Tony (2001) Romeo and Juliet *Broadsheet* Vol 12, Issue 3

Hall, Peter (1985) (adaptor) *George Orwell's Animal Farm* Methuen

Hazelwood, Patrick (2005) A Curriculum for the Love of Learning: one school's attempt to raise standards by returning to teaching children how to learn, rather than follow the rigid pathway laid down by the National Curriculum *Journal for Drama in Education*, vol 2, issue 2

Hayter, Sparkle (2002) *Naked Brunch* No Exit Press

Heathcote, Dorothy (Spring 2005) Contexts for Active Learning *Journal for Drama in Education*, vol.19, issue 1

Holstun Lopez, Barry (1995) *Of Wolves and Men* Simon and Schuster

Hulson, Maggie (1991) In Whose Image? *Theatre and Education Journal* issue no. 4

Hulson, Maggie (2002) The Priests – Sequencing the Class Experience *The Journal for Drama in Education* vol.19, issue 1

Johnson, Liz and O'Neil, Cecily (eds) (1985) *Dorothy Heathcote. Collected Writings on Education and Drama* Hutchinson

Kozulin, Alex (1998) *Psychological Tools A Sociocultural Approach to Education* Harvard University Press

Lang, Andrew (mcmvii) *Tales of Troy and Greece* Faber

Lucretius (50BC) trans. Martin Ferguson Smith (1969) *On the Nature of Things* Indianapolis

McEntagart, Tag (1981) Play and Theatre *SCYPT Journal* no.7 Standing Conference for Young People's Theatre

Mitchell, Stephen (2004) *Gilgamesh – A new English Version* Profile Books

Munch, Edvard *The Scream* in Oxford and Cambridge and RSA Examinations (2003) *Drama Practical Examination: Realisation Test* General Certificate of Secondary Education Oxford and Cambridge and RSA

Oxford and Cambridge and RSA Examinations *Drama* General Certificate of Education, Oxford and Cambridge and RSA Examinations

Oxford and Cambridge and RSA Examinations *Expressive Arts* General Certificate of Secondary Education Oxford and Cambridge and RSA Examinations

Oxford and Cambridge and RSA Examinations (2003) *Drama Practical Examination: Realisation Test* General Certificate of Secondary Education Oxford and Cambridge and RSA Examinations

Pinter, Harold (1988) *Mountain Language* in Pinter, Harold (1988/1996) *Mountain Language and Ashes to Ashes* Faber and Faber

Rosen, Michael (2004) *William Shakespeare, in his times, for our times* Redwords

Roy, Arundhati 2002 Shall We Leave it to the Experts? in *Another World is Possible* % attac

Smith, Dennis (2002) *Report from Ground Zero* Doubleday

Soanes, Catherine and Stevenson, Angus (2004) *Concise Oxford English Dictionary* Eleventh edition Oxford University Press

Stenhouse, Lawrence (1975) *An Introduction to Curriculum Research and Development* Heinemann

Thompson, Paul (1975) *The Children's Crusade* in Oxford and Cambridge and RSA Examinations (2003) Drama Practical Examination: Realisation Test General Certificate of Secondary Education Oxford and Cambridge and RSA

Vygotsky, LS (1981) quoted in Daniels, H (1996) (ed) *An Introduction to Vygotsky* Routledge

Wertenbaker, Timberlake (1996) *The Love of a Nightingale* in Timberlake Wertenbaker: *Plays* Faber and Faber

Wood, Michael (1985,1996) *In Search of the Trojan War* 2001 edition, BBC Worldwide Limited

Music, Videos and Websites
Music

Bogle, Eric *The Band Played Waltzing Matilda* on Tabor, June *Anthology* (MCCD 126) Music Club

Near, Holly and Gilbert, Ronnie *Harriet Tubman* on *Lifeline* Redwood Records

Gabriel, Peter (2002) CD *Long Walk Home* Realworld (Music from the film *Rabbit Proof Fence*)

Holiday, Billie tape *The Billie Holiday Songbook* Polygram 1985

Videos

Morris, Desmond *The Human Animal* BBC

Charlotte Uhlenbroek, (2004) presenting *Talking with Animals*, a series on BBC1 exploring the world of animal communication.

Websites

http://www.bbc.co.uk/nature/programmes/tv/talking with wolves

http://www.antislavery.org/homepage/antislavery/modern.htm